Garden Answers

Ponds and
water features

hamlyn

Garden Answers

Ponds and water features

Expert answers to all your questions

Richard Bird

First published in Great Britain in 2002 by Hamlyn,
a division of Octopus Publishing Group Limited,
2-4 Heron Quays,
London E14 4JP

Copyright © 2002 Octopus Publishing Group Limited

Distributed in the United States and Canada by
Sterling Publishing Co., Inc.
387 Park Avenue South
New York, NY 10016-8810

ISBN 0 600 60408 X

British Library Cataloguing-in-Publication Data
A catalogue record for this book is available from the British
Library

Printed and bound in China
10 9 8 7 6 5 4 3 2 1

NOTE
The Publishers cannot accept any legal responsibility or liability for
accidents or damage arising from the carrying out of any of the projects. In
addition, the Publishers recommend that any electrical work outdoors
should be carried out by a qualified electrician.

Contents

Introduction

Ever since gardens were first created water has played a part in their design. Water adds new dimensions to a garden, providing sound, reflections and movement, and the constant play of light and shadow moving over the surrounding plants and across nearby walls and fences is endlessly fascinating. Moving water, in the form of a stream or as water disturbed by fountains or waterfalls, creates even greater play of light and brings soothing and refreshing sounds to the garden.

The area around water is quite different from other areas in the garden. The plants are unlike their land-based equivalents in shape, form and colour, but as well as the plants growing in the water itself, there is a huge selection of plants that will grow in the pond's margins and in boggy ground, opening up new aspects of gardening. These plants are not only visually exciting but growing them can present the gardener with challenges and opportunities to experiment that do not exist with conventional garden plants.

Recent developments in materials and technology have made the building and installation of quite complex water features comparatively simple. Submersible pumps, flexible liners, geotexile matting and preformed units mean that it is possible to create ponds and associated fountains, streams, cascades and waterfalls to suit any style of garden, from formal to informal, and from large to small. It is even possible to buy kits, complete with everything you need to make bubble or millstone fountains. Garden centres and aquatic specialists provide everything that you need, and many suppliers operate mail order services on the internet.

Ponds are not difficult to construct, and they need surprisingly little maintenance when they have been built. Most gardeners are quite capable of building one or constructing a small water feature, and they are mostly completely trouble free. Occasionally, however, problems arise with the construction of the pond or the plants and wildlife associated with it. This book asks the questions that gardeners are likely to pose and answers them in a practical way, illustrating the points with artworks and photographs. The book falls into two main sections: the first looks at aspects of the design and construction of ponds and water features, and the second covers problems that arise with maintenance and repair. Although problems have been grouped and topics are tackled in a logical way, there is inevitably some overlap, and the index should be used to identify all questions on a particular subject. For example, if you are interested in creating a formal pond, you will find information about the design, planting, construction and maintenance in different sections; looking under 'formal ponds' in the index will direct you to the relevant pages.

1 Getting Started

Initial planning and costs

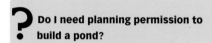
Do I need planning permission to build a pond?

Probably not, although it may depend on where you live as well as on factors such as the size of the intended pond. There is so much variation from area to area and country to country that if you are at all uncertain the only absolutely safe approach is to check with your local planning authority before you begin work. If you do go ahead without permission and are then forced to fill in your pond it will have been an expensive and time-consuming exercise. It would also be sensible to contact your water authority or supplier, especially if you are creating a large pond or lake that you would like to supply from a nearby stream.

In some areas restrictions are imposed on the use of water, especially in prolonged periods of drought. Local bans on the use of garden hoses might prevent you from filling or refilling a pond, although in some regions it might be possible to top up the water level during periods of restriction if the pond supports wildlife. Alternatively, you may be allowed to fill the pond only if the mains water is metered.

Is it easy to make a pond?

One of the joys of introducing a water feature into the garden is that it can be as straightforward or as complicated as you like.

One of the simplest things you can do is to sink an inverted dustbin lid into a lawn so that the rim is level with the surface of the grass. Place a large pebble or stone in the centre and fill the lid with water to make a miniature pond. On the other hand, if you have space, you can use a digger to create a lake tens or even hundreds of metres (yards) across.

Between the two extremes is a wide range of possibilities, the majority of which are well within the capabilities of most gardeners. Most are based on the principle of digging a hole and lining it in some way. The digging is relatively straightforward as long you have the strength; the main problem is the disposal of the soil taken from the hole (see pages 34–5). The ease or otherwise of lining the hole depends very much on the material you choose. A rigid, preformed liner is fairly easy; a flexible liner is moderately difficult but well within the competence of most gardeners; a shaped concrete pond will call for more skills but will still be within the capabilities of most gardeners with some practical DIY abilities.

? I would like a pond but do not have much money. What possibilities are there?

It is possible to make a pond from a small, waterproof container, which may not cost you anything at all, although you might want to spend some money on attractive water plants. However, if you want a larger feature you will probably have to buy a liner of some

The relative costs of ponds

The following materials can be used to make a pond; they are listed from the least to the most expensive for a similar area of surface water:

- Small, free-standing container
- Puddled clay (if free clay is available)
- Polythene sheeting
- Rigid, preformed unit
- PVC
- Low density polythene (LDPE)
- Butyl rubber
- Concrete

Remember that it is always preferable to have a smaller pond with better materials than a large pond with cheap materials. It will last longer, cause fewer problems and probably look more attractive.

kind, and it is worth bearing in mind that the cheaper the liner, the less durable it will be. Polythene is the cheapest lining material, but it also has the shortest life. However, if you use it to line the hole and then cover it with a layer of fine soil (make sure there are no stones that might puncture the liner) to protect it from ultraviolet light it may last for several years. In general, however, buying a cheap liner is a false economy.

If you are fortunate enough (in this context) to have clay in your garden you could use it to make a natural pond. A puddled clay pond made from clay from your own garden will not cost anything (except effort) as long as you do everything yourself. However, if you need to buy in the clay the price could rise sharply (see pages 46–7).

Rather than trying to create a large pond on a shoestring and making an unattractive and short-lived job of it, it would be better to scale things down and create something you can afford.

Practical considerations

? Do I need to take services such as electricity and the water supply into account when I build a pond?

Your decision about the siting of your pond should not depend on the position of the domestic water and electricity supplies, although you should find out if any mains pipes run across your garden so that you can avoid them when you excavate the hole. If necessary, the services can be run from the house to the pond.

All ponds need water, of course, but after the initial filling the water level can be topped up with rainwater from roofs or, if it needs topping up with mains water, it is likely that a garden hose run from the house will be sufficient. It is most unlikely that you will have to organize a separate, permanent supply.

An electricity supply will not be required for a simple pond, but if you want to include a pump, filter or lights, a power supply will be essential and you should consider laying a permanent cable (*illustrated below*). A mains

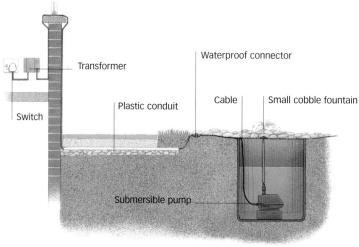

Using low-voltage electricity

A low-voltage system can be used to operate a cobble fountain or pond lighting

Transformer
Waterproof connector
Plastic conduit
Cable
Small cobble fountain
Switch
Submersible pump

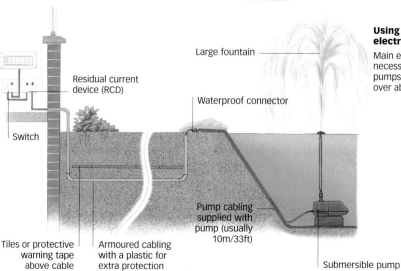

Using mains electricity

Main electricity is necessary to operate pumps for fountains over about 1m (3ft)

Large fountain
Residual current device (RCD)
Waterproof connector
Switch
Tiles or protective warning tape above cable
Armoured cabling with a plastic for extra protection
Pump cabling supplied with pump (usually 10m/33ft)
Submersible pump

supply involves laying special cabling in a protective, armoured sleeve in a trench at least 60cm (2ft) deep; it also involves installing a residual current device (RCD) in case the cable is accidentally severed. A low-voltage system, which will be adequate for most small water features, requires the installation of a transformer to step down the mains current to 12 volts.

 Our water supply is metered. Can we have a pond?

There is no reason you should not have a pond, and there are generally no restrictions on using mains water to fill a pond. If you fill the pond once and then only occasionally use mains water to top it up, it should not be prohibitively expensive. When your water is metered, however, you have to pay for every drop you use, and you would not choose to create a stream with water running permanently from the mains (this would, in any case, be a tremendous waste of water, whether it was metered or not). You should also make sure that there are no leaks in your pond, which would mean that it required regular topping up (see pages 132–3). To replace losses through evaporation divert into the pond all the rainwater from your roofs and from areas, such as patios and drives, that have hard surfaces.

Safety first

It cannot be said too often that water and electricity are a dangerous and potentially fatal combination. Install waterproof, armoured cables and use waterproof connectors. Always employ a qualified electrician to advise on the layout of the system and to install the fittings for your water feature.

Saving water

So that you do not have to add too much mains water:

- Mend any leaks as soon as you notice them;
- Make sure that the top of the pond is perfectly level all round;
- Capture as much water as possible from roofs and hard surfaces within your garden;
- Cover some of the water surface with waterlilies to reduce evaporation;
- Resist the temptation to use the pond as a convenient place to fill up watering cans.

 Is there an optimum size of pond?

Although the short reply is 'probably not', it is important that the pond is in proportion to your garden and house and to other features in the garden. Like the other features in your garden, the pond should balance the space in which it is situated. Ponds that are too large for the garden are not easy to disguise, although a small pond can be surrounded by plants or even objects so that its size is not immediately obvious. There is no rule of thumb. Try a combination of drawing a rough plan and marking the outline of the pond on the ground so that you can stand back and try to visualize how it will eventually look. Bear in mind that it can be more difficult to establish a good balance in a small volume of water, and a surface area of about 6sq m (65sq ft) with a depth of 70–75cm (28–30in) in one part of the pond will provide a suitable habitat for a range of plants and animals. If you want to keep fish in your pond the surface area will have a direct effect on the stocking rate (see page 18 and 102–3).

Siting and orientation

Putting a pond just anywhere could be disastrous for the appearance of your garden, and it is important to consider the position of the pond in relation not only to the other features but also to the house. Although the pond will be artificial, in the sense that it is entirely manmade, it must fit into your overall garden as naturally as possible. If you have a formal garden, your pond should also be formal. In an informal garden, the pond should have an informal, irregular shape, or, if you want an informal garden but already have a formal pond, the edges should be disguised and blurred by planting so that it fits into your new scheme. Similarly, if the garden is designed for wildlife, a formal, unplanted, concrete pond would be wholly inappropriate.

Most ponds are best sited in sun, although in most gardens it is likely that there will be a little shade, perhaps at one end of a pond or perhaps caused by the moving sun. In general, however, it is best to avoid putting a pond entirely in the shade.

On the whole, trees are not good companions for ponds. If you have a large pond you will probably get away with one or even two trees if they do not cast too much shadow (in the northern hemisphere, this means they should be on the north side of the pond). A pond that is surrounded by trees so that sunlight cannot penetrate to the water is likely to be a dead pond because the underwater plants that supply vital oxygen need sunlight to function. In addition, the leaves of deciduous trees will fall into the pond in autumn and will slowly rot, producing harmful gases, and evergreen trees shed leaves all year round, which will also decompose to the detriment of the water. If you want a successful pond you will have to remove some of the trees to allow in some sunlight.

No; the position of the pond within the garden will be determined by the shape of the garden. The edges of a straight-sided pond will usually be parallel or at right angles to the boundaries of the garden. A round pond has no orientation as such, but for an oval pond you should take the axis through its length as the starting point when you are considering

Where to site your pond

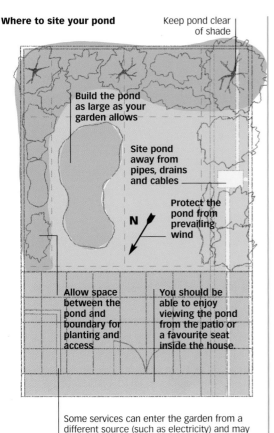

Keep pond clear of shade

Build the pond as large as your garden allows

Site pond away from pipes, drains and cables

Protect the pond from prevailing wind

N

Allow space between the pond and boundary for planting and access

You should be able to enjoy viewing the pond from the patio or a favourite seat inside the house.

Some services can enter the garden from a different source (such as electricity) and may make right angle turns

narrow pond it may look better if it runs down the length of the garden (*illustrated below*) rather than cutting the plot in half, but even this guideline may be broken if, for example, your garden is on two levels. Position the pond so that it gets the maximum sun, but otherwise the overriding concern should be that it fits in with the overall garden design.

its position. The irregular shape of an informal pond and many semi-formal ponds means that you do not need to worry about the orientation. If you are building a long, fairly

Siting a pond

Resist the temptation of positioning the pond in the lowest point in your garden. Such areas are not only often in a frost pocket, which will limit the range of plants you can include in your pond, but a low-lying pond might be susceptible to run-off from higher ground elsewhere in the garden, including chemicals, which will encourage algal growth even if they don't kill everything else.

 From what position is a pond best viewed?

This depends largely on the general layout of the garden. Because the pond is usually the most interesting feature in a garden, it should not be so totally enclosed with vegetation that it is hidden from view. If the pond cannot be viewed from the patio, consider creating a sitting area nearby, where you can relax and watch what is going on. Much time is spent in the house looking out, especially in winter, so it makes sense to position the pond so that it can be seen from the most often-used room, whether this is a sitting room or a kitchen. When you are planning the pond, make sure that there is a clear sight of the water by excluding plants from along the line of vision.

Sloping gardens and unusual sites

? The only suitable place in my garden for a pond is on sloping ground. Can I build it there?

A sloping site can be an excellent place for a pond because it gives you an opportunity to create a water feature on different levels, and you can be creative and even have a system of cascades, waterfalls and streams or steps (*illustrated above*). Such a scheme will obviously involve a lot more work and will probably be more expensive than a water feature on a flat site. A free-standing pond, with no associated features, will have to be partly excavated into the slope and partly built up on the slope so that the tops of the sides are level all round. On a very steep slope it may be sensible to get professional advice, particularly if you are building on a large scale, because there is always the danger of the slope slipping. Instead of creating one large pond, which

might be difficult on steeply sloping ground without a great deal of engineering work, you could make several small ones. A series of ponds that do not disturb the ground too much should be within the capabilities of most gardeners, and you could also integrate them into a rock garden.

? A stream runs through my garden. Can I make use of it?

Although many gardeners would love to have a natural stream running through their gardens, it can be a problem if it floods or if it is in the wrong place, because it will be difficult or even impossible to divert. You may be able to add a pond next to it, but you must seek advice from your local planning authority and your water supplier before you do this in case the changes you make affect the amount of water that is delivered downstream. You should always check with the relevant government agency before making any changes to water flowing through your garden.

You do not, however, need permission to grow a wide variety of interesting plants along the banks (*illustrated below left*). You may prefer to leave it natural by growing native species, or you might adopt a more decorative approach and use some of the wide range of water and waterside plants that are now available (see pages 92–3).

? The only place I can build a pond is near the house. Will that cause any problems?

Building a pond near your house will probably cause no problems unless you want a deep pond. A shallow pond, as long as it is not positioned right up against the house walls,

Sloping ground

Sloping ground often has a rocky substratum quite close to the surface. Before you finally decide on the position of your pond, dig one or two trial holes to check that there is enough soil for you to be able to excavate to a sufficient depth.

should not lead to any difficulties. If you want a pond that is close to the house consider building a raised one, with a brick or stone surround, rather than digging it into the ground. Never create a pond immediately next to a house wall because this will cause all kinds of damp problems on the inside of the house. Nor should you fix a waterspout or fountain against a house wall: no matter how carefully you prepare the wall, some damp will penetrate. If you are in any doubt as to the wisdom of placing a pond near your house seek professional advice. It is better to spend some money initially rather than a lot of money putting problems right.

Choosing a water feature

? **Is one style of pond more appropriate for a particular type of garden than another?**

This is not easy to answer, simply because there are so many types of garden and so many types of pond. There are a few guidelines to follow during the initial planning stage, but, as with most gardening 'rules', they are there to be broken. A formal pond will always look best in a formal garden. Its clean lines and simplicity suit the formal, often symmetrical surroundings, in which a wilder pond would look completely out of place. If the garden is less formal, either in its deliberate overall design or simply because the gardener prefers somewhere with a more 'lived-in' appearance, an informal pond will be a better choice. If you like to watch birds and want to encourage other wildlife to your garden, a pool built for their needs will be the one to choose, although wildlife will visit other types of ponds. In a small garden a feature

Enhancing reflections
If you have a small pond, especially one in a courtyard garden, consider positioning a mirror next to the pond so that you not only produce many more reflections but also apparently double the size of the pond. If you wish, disguise the edges of the mirror by surrounding it with plants.

such as a waterspout or pebble fountain dribbling into a container will be all that there is room for. As with other aspects of your garden design, make a list of all your requirements and choose the type of pool most appropriate to your needs, to the size of your garden and to your pocket.

? **Reflections from water are beautiful. Should I build a feature with still or moving water?**

Running water is dynamic and has the advantage of producing a continually changing pattern of reflections. Whether the water

takes the form of a stream, fountain or waterfall, it has the advantage that it produces sound, which can be an additional reason for wanting a feature with moving water. Still water, on the other hand, provides a more slowly changing pattern, as it moves gently up and down as well as reflecting the gradually changing position of the sun. A still pond can be enlivened by introducing a fountain or by having a waterfall tumble into it.

The reflective properties of water are not much good without something to reflect, and surrounding the feature, whether the water is still or moving, with plants will enhance the play of water as it moves. The varying surfaces, shapes and textures of marginal and water plants will add to the quality of the reflections and the interest that they create.

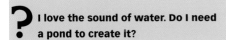

? I love the sound of water. Do I need a pond to create it?

No, you do not. Sound comes from the movement of water, and you can have a fountain (*illustrated below right*) without a pond as long as you have sufficient space to accommodate a sump or reservoir that will house a submersible pump and contain the water that is recirculated. One of the most popular types of water feature is the pebble or millstone fountain, which involves water from a hidden reservoir being forced up, over the decorative stones and then sinking back into the reservoir below, from where it is recirculated by a small pump. Wall-mounted waterspouts work on a similar principle. These small features also provide the pleasant murmur of moving water.

Types of water feature

Each style can vary in size and scope, and features can be combined if space and funds allow.

- Formal ponds
- Informal ponds
- Semi-formal ponds
- Wildlife pools
- Container ponds
- Bog gardens
- Streams
- Waterspouts or fountains

Suiting the water feature to the garden

? What kind of pond would be best for fish?

Provided the water is oxygenated you will be able to stock even a small pond with fish. The usual recommended stocking rate is to have one fish 5cm (2in) long (from nose to tail) for every 30 x 30cm (1 x 1ft) of surface water, and to sustain fish the pond should contain submerged oxygenating, plants. In addition to an adequate surface area, most fish will do better if the pond contains at least one deep section where the water temperature will remain fairly constant all year round (see also pages 102–3).

Fish-breeders, especially those interested in koi, will prefer to build special ponds, which are more like holding tanks than attractive garden features.

? What water feature could I have in a courtyard garden?

Because courtyard gardens are usually small and paved, there is rarely space for a conventional pond, at least not one of any size. There are, however, several possible water features that will enhance the appearance of the courtyard and add to your enjoyment of your garden (*illustrated below*). The first possibility is to think small and create a miniature pond, perhaps no more than 60–100cm (2–3ft) across. This could be a free-standing container or a built feature with a stone or brick surround. Waterproof half-barrels, which are attractive in their own right, make excellent small ponds. A built-in pond could be sunk wholly or partly into the ground if it is possible to remove some of the existing

Plants for a small pond

Although most waterlilies are far too large for a small container, there are some miniature cultivars (see pages 86–7). Among the other plants suitable for a small pond are:

- *Acorus gramineus* 'Pusillus' (dwarf Japanese rush)
- *Damasonium alisma* (starfruit)
- *Eleocharis acicularis* (hair grass)
- *Fontinalis antipyretica* (willow moss, water moss)
- *Houttuynia cordata*
- *Isolepis cernua* (mop sedge)
- *Juncus effusus* f. *spiralis* (corkscrew rush)
- *Myosotis scorpioides* (syn. *M. palustris*; water forget-me-not)
- *Typha minima*
- *Wolffia arrhiza*

hard surface, or, if necessary, it could be built entirely above ground level, with a surround of brick, stone or even railway sleepers. There are plenty of small water plants that will live perfectly happily in a small pond without overpowering it. Another possibility is to think vertically. A waterspout, fixed to a wall or some other structure (*illustrated right*), can trickle water down into a container of some sort, which again can be entirely below ground or be an ornamental bowl. Such a feature will take up only a little space but will be an attractive addition to your garden, as the sounds, sparkle and moisture create a cool, tranquil environment.

? **Can I build a formal pond in a small garden?**

You can build a formal pond in any size of garden as long as you get the proportions right. A large pool that fills a small garden will look wrong, but a small pool in a small garden will look fine, even if the pond is no more than 60cm (2ft) across. There is no reason why you should not use several small ponds, perhaps in a pattern in a small area, and such an arrangement will work better in a gravel or paved garden than one put down to grass.

? **Can I have a stream in a town garden?**

It is possible to have a stream anywhere as long as it fits in with the surroundings. In a small, paved courtyard garden, for example, you can create a stream in a narrow rill or channel, no more than 15cm (6in) wide, that runs between paving stones. It could be straight, arranged in a geometric pattern., If there was no paving, a stream could be built in a sinuous pattern. A more natural stream could be a rock garden, with the stream flowing between an upper and a lower pool.

? **I would like to create a natural-looking garden. Can I build an informal pond in a town garden?**

There is no reason at all why you should not do this. Indeed, there are many reasons why you should create such a pond. There are far fewer differences between 'town gardens' and 'country gardens' than most people realize, and there is frequently no difference at all in size, because many new village gardens are as small as or even smaller than town gardens.

Natural ponds are designed to appeal to wildlife rather than to be pretty, although there is no reason why they should not be attractive as well. In towns (and increasingly often in the country) there is a shortage of natural habitats for all kinds of creatures, and by creating a pond where there is natural food and vegetation you will be increasing the range of habitats in your area and the amount of wildlife that can be supported there (see pages 26–7).

not conventionally 'pond-shaped' but takes the form of a rill, a long, narrow strip only about 15cm (6in) wide. A rill may be straight or curved, perhaps into a spiral.

Formal ponds

? What is a formal pond?

A formal pond is a feature whose overall shape is as important as the water and what lies within it. The most usual shape for a formal pond is regular and geometric – squares, rectangles, circles or ovals, for example – and the lines are clear-cut and the edges unmasked by tumbling plants. Such a pond is usually part of a formally designed garden, and its shape plays an important part in the design and layout of the garden as a whole, reinforcing the symmetry of the scheme. Such a pond usually, but not exclusively, has a hard surround, such as paving. Sometimes a formal water feature is

? What kind of setting is best for a formal pond?

A formal pond will always look best in a formal setting. Such gardens are generally laid out on a symmetrical basis, but even when the setting is irregular, there will be a cleanliness of line that can be seen as formal.

The garden is often reduced to a minimum, with only a little planting, such as low box hedges and tightly clipped trees or bushes at regular intervals. Rhythm plays an important part in a formal garden, and even in the pond the planting is controlled, perhaps by being limited to symmetrical plantings of a single species in each corner (*illustrated right*). It would also be possible to have a formal pond in one section of the garden, perhaps designed as a formal courtyard that is screened off from the rest of the garden, which is generally rather more informal in character.

? Is a minimum depth of water necessary in a formal pool?

A formal pool is usually of an even depth across the width and length. If marginal planting is to be included, ledges may be built around the edges to vary the depth so that plants requiring different depths can be used. Formal pools are not usually very deep, but if you are using a liner aim for a depth of 60–90cm (2–3ft) so that the liner is not visible.

? Which plants can I include in a formal pond?

The key to a formal pond is to keep the planting restrained and limited to just a few species. The plants must not obscure the shape of the pool nor completely cover the surface, unless plants of the same height, such as waterlilies, are allowed to spread over the water. The plants are usually set out in a regular pattern, such as in the corners, or at fixed intervals down the length of the pool. Sometimes a single cluster of plants is all that is required. As with the shape of the pool, the planting should be crisp and clear cut. A few low plants, such as waterlilies, contrasted with a few vertical ones, such as irises or

Plants for a formal pond

When you are planting a formal pond, select one or two species and space them carefully to emphasize the overall shape and lines of the pond. The depth indicated is the depth of water above the growing point, not the overall depth of the pond.

- *Acorus calamus* (sweet flag, myrtle flag): 23cm (9in)
- *Butomus umbellatus* (flowering rush): 5–40cm (2–16in)
- *Eleocharis acicularis* (hair grass): submerged
- *Glyceria maxima* var. *variegata* (syn. *G. aquatica* var. *variegata*; variegated water grass): 15cm (6in)
- *Iris laevigata*: 8–10cm (3–4in)
- *Nymphaea* cvs. (waterlily): various
- *Peltandra sagittifolia* (syn. *P. alba*; white arrow arum): 5–8cm (2–3in)
- *Saururus cernuus* (water dragon, lizard's tail): 10–15cm (4–6in)
- *Schoenoplectus lacustris* subsp. *tabernaemontani* 'Zebrinus' (zebra rush): 8–15cm (3–6in)

reeds, will be most successful. Plants like hostas and ferns, with gracefully arching leaves, can be used in pots around the pool rather than in it, but they should be positioned so that they do not obscure the lines of the pool and allow its formality to be lost.

as fountains or a cascade or waterfall, may be built into the pond, and the surroundings could include annual bedding plants. Preformed, rigid pools are ideal for this type of pond.

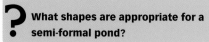

? What shapes are appropriate for a semi-formal pond?

A semi-formal pond can be any shape you like, from the regular, geometric outlines of a formal pond to the sinuous, random curves of an informal one. If you choose a regular shape the formality is likely to be lost among the planting, which will disguise or hide some of the edges. If you prefer an irregular shape, the outline will be more apparent than with an informal pond because the edges will be more exposed. There is no need to make the shape more complicated than necessary, and the more regular the shape the easier it will be to line with a flexible liner. Many of the rigid, preformed pools, which are broadly kidney-shaped, are the perfect shape for this kind of pond.

Semi-formal ponds

? What is a semi-formal pond?

A semi-formal pond is, as the name suggests, one that is halfway between a formal pool and an informal one. It is the type of pond you might create in the middle of a lawn or next to a patio. It is likely that the greater part, if not all, of its edges will be visible, but the shape will be informal rather than geometric. Such a pond belongs in a neat, tidy garden, where everything has its place but not to the point where everything is ordered and symmetrical, as in a formal garden. The pond will not depend on its shape for its interest in quite the same way a formal pond does, but it will be less densely planted than an informal one, and the balance will be in favour of the pond rather than the plants, with a large part of the surface kept clear of plants so that any fish can be clearly seen. Other features, such

? Is it necessary to have a minimum depth of water?

Although it is possible to have a pond with water that is only 15cm (6in) deep, the best ponds are undoubtedly much deeper than this. As a rule, the pond should be sufficiently deep that the bottom cannot be seen when the pond is full, which means that you should aim for a minimum of at least 60cm (2ft). It is always a good idea to create a pond with a range of depths so that you can accommodate plants that require different depths of water as well as giving wildlife a range of habitats. Shallow water is warmer in summer but will freeze more quickly in winter, and although deeper water is colder it provides a haven for fish in very hot weather and a hiding place from predators such as herons.

Plants for a semi-formal pond

The following plants are appropriate for a semi-formal or informal pond. The dimension indicated is the depth of water above the crown of the plant, not the depth of the pond.

- *Caltha palustris* (marsh marigold, kingcup): to 23cm (9in)
- *Houttuynia cordata* 'Chameleon' (syn. *H. cordata* 'Tricolor'): to 5cm (2in)
- *Iris laevigata*: 8–10cm (3–4in)
- *Iris pseudacorus* (yellow flag, flag iris): to 30cm (1ft)
- *Myriophyllum spicatum* (spiked milfoil): submerged
- *Myosotis scorpioides* (syn. *M. palustris*; water forget-me-not): to 15cm (6in)
- *Nymphaea* cvs. (waterlily): various
- *Orontium aquaticum* (golden club): 30cm (1ft)
- *Pontederia cordata* (pickerel weed): to 13cm (5in)
- *Ranunculus lingua* (greater spearwort): 8–15cm (3–6in), illustrated left

Informal ponds

What is an informal pond?

Informal ponds are not necessarily untidy, but they have a relaxed atmosphere about them. The edges are usually obscured in places so that the shape is not obvious. Water may disappear under sweeping shrubs, so that the bank is not visible, giving the impression that the water continues into the distance. Such a pond will have plenty of planting around it, and the plants will be as important visually as the water. Although there should be some open stretches of the bank where the water can be clearly seen, especially from sitting areas or from the house, from some directions only a sparkle of water, glinting among the vegetation, will hint at the presence of the pond.

What shape is best for an informal pond?

There is no fixed shape for an informal pond, but, as the name suggests, it should not be a regular, geometric shape. Instead, it should have sinuous, curved edges. Do not make an outline with narrow or pointed inlets, which rarely look natural and are, in any case, difficult to line neatly. A smooth, continuous curve is more appropriate and easier to make and maintain. Because the actual shape will be blurred by planting around and in the pond the exact shape is not particularly important.

What kind of garden is best for an informal pond?

An informal pond will suit a garden where there are plenty of borders and plants, with drifts of herbaceous perennials and shrubs blending into each other. Informal ponds are often set in grass, which is an appropriate edging (see pages 54–5), although they can be bordered on one side by a path. An informal pond rarely looks right if it is set in an area of hard surfacing, such as paving or gravel, nor should it be isolated, even in grass. Instead, plants should be grown right down to the water's edge, with perhaps a shrub or two overhanging part of the edge, although the branches should not be allowed to hang over too much of the water's surface.

❓ Is there a minimum depth of water that is necessary in an informal pond?

As with all ponds, the aim should be to make the pond so deep that the bottom is not visible, and it is sensible to vary the depth, with marginal ledges about 23cm (9in) deep and a deeper central section to at least 60cm (2ft), so that the pond is suitable for growing a wide range of plants as well as giving fish and other wildlife a variety of habitats.

❓ What percentage of the water surface can be taken up with vegetation?

Although an informal pool will have plenty of planting in and around it, aim to keep at least some of the margins clear of vegetation, with

Removing excess vegetation

Clear areas of vegetation from the pond at least once or twice in the summer by pulling it out with a rake. The plants are rich in nutrients, so put them in the compost bin. Make sure that you do not puncture or damage the liner as you work.

clear water going right up to the bank. Similarly, do not allow the surface to become completely covered with floating plants (*illustrated above*). Cut back waterlilies and other floating plants so that at least half of the surface area is clear of vegetation.

❓ I have an informal pond. What are the best plants for it?

Any of the plants suggested for a semi-formal pond will be appropriate in an informal pond (see pages 22–3). Although you could limit the planting to a single species, it will be more interesting to have a combination of foliage and flowering plants as well as a mixture of shapes and textures. Tall marginals, such as irises, non-invasive forms of *Typha* (bulrush) and *Carex* (sedge), can be combined with lower growing, wide-leaved foliaged plants, such as *Calla palustris* (bog arum) and *Zantedeschia aethiopica* (arum lily, calla lily), with some floating plants, such as waterlilies, to finish off the picture. Low-growing plants, such as *Mimulus luteus* (monkey musk) and *Myosotis scorpioides* (water forget-me-not), can be allowed to weave among the marginal planting to bind them together.

Wildlife ponds

 What is a wildlife pond?

A wildlife pond is designed and built especially for wildlife. Birds and other animals will be attracted to any water, but it is possible to create a pond that will include features that make life easier and more pleasing for them. Security from predators is important, so a wildlife pond will have plenty of cover around the banks and in the water. If the pond is large enough nesting places can be included. Plants in and around the pond will be a source of food for a range of birds, as will insects and other small animals attracted to the pond. A wildlife pond will almost certainly be informal in shape and design, and will often contain native plants, rather than hybridized cultivars. Garden plants will play a part in the scheme, but will be those that are rich in nectar and pollen, which excludes many of the brightly coloured, modern hybrids. Although it is rewarding to watch everything that is going on in a wildlife pond, the purpose of creating the pond is to help wildlife, and so there should be some areas that are not open to view.

Requirements for a wildlife pond

If you are serious about creating a pond specifically for wildlife, you must provide:

- A secure site
- Plenty of nearby cover
- Easy access in and out of the pond
- Areas of open water
- Oxygenating plants in the water
- Food plants in and by the water

 Can I keep fish in a wildlife pond?

Although a wildlife pond may seem to be the obvious place for fish, remember that most fish are omnivorous, which will eat plants and other animals. If there are a lot of fish in your pond they can virtually eliminate other small creatures, such as dragonfly larvae, and frog- or toadspawn, and populations of tadpoles can be reduced or completely wiped out by greedy fish. In many ways it is best not to introduce ornamental fish into a natural pond if you want to have a wide diversity of wildlife. A large pond, or one with plenty of different

Wildlife pond

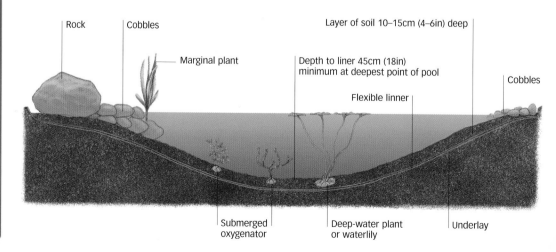

Rock | Cobbles | Layer of soil 10–15cm (4–6in) deep

Marginal plant | Depth to liner 45cm (18in) minimum at deepest point of pool

Flexible linner | Cobbles

Submerged oxygenator | Deep-water plant or waterlily | Underlay

Plants for a wildlife pond

These plants are among those appropriate for planting in and around a wildlife pond. The dimension given is the depth of water above the crown of the plant.

- *Carex pendula* (pendulous sedge): 2.5cm (1in)
- *Iris pseudacorus* (yellow flag, flag iris): to 30cm (1ft)
- *Lemna trisulca* (ivy-leaved duckweed): floating
- *Ludwigia palustris* (water purslane): 15–30cm (6–12in)
- *Menyanthes trifoliata* (bog bean, marsh trefoil): to 5cm (2in)
- *Phragmites australis* (syn. *P. communis*; common reed): 8cm (3in)
- *Rumex hydrolapathum* (great water dock): to 15cm (6in)
- *Typha angustifolia* (narrow-leaved reedmace): to 40cm (16in)

habitats and hiding places, will support a small population of fish without too many problems. Native fish are more suitable than introduced species, such as goldfish or koi.

 What type of plants can I grow in my wildlife garden?

If you wanted to be a purist you would limit your choice to native plants that grow in your locality. However, this approach is unrealistic and restrictive. First, by introducing a wider range of plants you will be offering a diversity of foodstuffs and cover. Second, although some native pond plants are beautiful, many are little more than weeds. Compromise and draw up a list of plants that will satisfy both you and the wildlife. Bear in mind that some garden plants are inappropriate for any pond: only water plants should be planted in the water. The banks of a pond are usually more like conventional beds, but in a wildlife garden many bedding plants would be inappropriate as they have nothing to offer wildlife. They are often sterile, producing no seed for birds and mammals to eat, and many of them do not provide nectar or pollen for insects. Try to use plants that provide cover or food or that will provide a natural, attractive background against which the wildlife can be seen.

 Is any particular shape best for a wildlife pond?

A wildlife pond can be any shape you like, and the animals that will frequent it will be unaffected by aesthetic considerations. On the whole, however, a formal pond is usually too bleak for much wildlife, apart from ornamental fish, because there is little planting in it. An informal shape, with gently curving sides, will seem more fitting. More important than the horizontal shape of the surface is the vertical shape or profile of the pond. If possible, it should vary in depth from shallow areas to some comparatively deep places so that there is a wider range of habitats than is possible in a flat-bottomed pool. Some animals prefer to spawn in shallow water, which is not only warmer than deeper water but is often free from predating fish. Some bottom-feeding fish, on the other hand, prefer to hide in deep water, safely away from the prying eyes of herons and other predators. A wildlife pond is, therefore, more likely to be made with a flexible liner or from puddled clay than from concrete or a preformed unit.

Bog gardens

? **What is a bog garden?**

A bog garden is an area of soil that is waterlogged or even wet all year round. It is similar to, but not, strictly, the same as, an area of moist soil such as might be found close to the shallow margins of an informal pool. Gardeners who are interested in growing a wide range of plants from different habitats like to create a separate bog garden so that they can grow some of the plants that thrive in those conditions. In some cases it is simply a matter of planting in the margins of a pond, but gardeners who do not necessarily want a pond or those who would like to grow more plants than can be accommodated around the pond will prefer to create a special area in which the soil is kept artificially moist. This is achieved by lining a bed with heavy-duty polythene or an old pond liner and then filling it in with a moisture-retentive soil. If the bog garden is created next to a pond, water from

the pond can be used to top up the water level in the bog garden. If a separate bog garden is built, it will need to be kept moist by a semi-automatic system or to be periodically flooded with a garden hose or with water that has run off from the house.

? **Can a bog garden be any shape?**

Yes; a bog garden is like any other bed in the garden. Ideally, however, the bog garden should be at least as wide as it is long because it will be easier to keep such an area moist. It is not only important that the soil is moist; bog plants like a moist atmosphere as well, and it is easier to achieve this among plants in a wide area than it is when they are set in a narrow strip. If you have space, a wide bed is preferable because many of the plants that can be grown in a bog garden can grow quite large, and tall plants in a narrow bed nearly always look unsatisfactory. An exception would be if you were to create long, narrow beds along the sides of a stream, but even here you should try to provide some additional width in places on at least one side.

? **Does a bog garden need to have areas of water in it?**

Natural bogs often have patches of visible water, but in the garden this is not essential. Indeed, it can be a nuisance, because not all of the plants grown in a bog garden will grow in standing water. They like moist conditions but will die if their roots are in stagnant water. Most bog gardens, therefore, are constructed in such a way that the soil is moisture-retentive but excess water can drain away. If you wanted to create an authentic bog, areas of water could be included, but they are best avoided in most gardens. A nearby or adjacent pond will be more attractive and just as useful.

Bog garden plants

The following are suitable for inclusion in a bog garden, although they would also grow in any reliably moist soil elsewhere in the garden.

- *Cardamine pratensis* (lady's smock, cuckoo flower)
- *Filipendula ulmaria* (meadowsweet), illustrated left
- *Gunnera manicata* (giant rhubarb)
- *Iris ensata* (syn. *I. kaempferi*)
- *Lobelia cardinalis* (cardinal flower, Indian pink)
- *Lythrum salicaria* (purple loosestrife)
- *Onoclea sensibilis* (sensitive fern)
- *Persicaria bistorta* (syn. *Polygonum bistorta*; bistort)
- *Primula japonica* (Japanese primrose)
- *Rodgersia pinnata*

Does a bog garden have to be built next to a pond?

No, although bog gardens do associate well with ponds. A large area of bog plants viewed across the surface of a pond will look very attractive, of course, because the water is a natural companion to a boggy area, both visually and in helping to keep the soil and atmosphere moist. Some bog gardens will also benefit if the pond is constructed so that excess water runs into the bog garden. However, it is not an essential partnership, and many successful bog gardens are created away from any water.

What kind of plants can I grow in a bog garden?

Several different groups of plants can be grown in a bog garden. First, there are the plants that are often grown in the shallow water around the margins of a pond. Although not all grow without standing water, most can be grown in ordinary soil as long as it is moist

– *Caltha palustris* (marsh marigold, kingcup) is a good example. Second, there are the true bog plants, which naturally grow in bogs and marshy ground – *Osmunda regalis* (royal fern, flowering fern) and *Trollius europaeus* (European globeflower), for example. Then there are those plants that can be grown in ordinary garden soil as long as it is moist. Such plants do not necessarily need a bog garden, but do well in the conditions found there. Hostas are a good example. Finally, there are one or two structural plants, such as trees and shrubs, which will grow in moist conditions – *Salix* spp. (willow), for example. These four categories cover a vast range of plants.

How do I plant bog plants?

Bog plants are planted in the conventional way: directly into the soil. Dig a hole in the soil and place the plant in the centre of it with its roots well spread out. The plant should be at the same depth that it was in its pot. Fill in the soil around and gently firm down. Do not press too hard or the soil will compact.

2 Building Your Pond

Materials and equipment

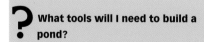

? What tools will I need to build a pond?

This will partly depend, of course, on the style and size of the proposed pond, but the following will be useful. In the first instance, you will need a hammer, pegs and string to mark out the outline of the pool. To get the levels correct you will need a long piece of wood (to act as a straight edge) and a spirit level. If you do not have a spirit level a water level can be used or, if you can find one, a translucent garden hose. The next problem is digging the pond. A spade will suffice for a small pond, but a mechanical digger will make life easier for anything larger. Small self-drive diggers can be hired *(illustrated right)* and you can even get one with a driver. You will need some means of getting rid of the spoil, which will at least mean a wheelbarrow, but you may also have to hire a waste-disposal skip to have it taken from your garden. A shovel will be useful for removing loose soil as well as for moving sand and mixing concrete. A garden rake will be needed for levelling the ground and removing stones. If any block-work is involved you will need a bricklayer's trowel as well as buckets for carrying cement. Sharp scissors or a sharp knife will be needed for cutting liners and underlay.

Tools and equipment

You will need some or all of the following to build a pond of any size. The items marked with an asterisk (*) will be needed for a large pond.

- Bricklayer's trowel
- Buckets
- Fork
- Garden hose
- Garden rake
- Hammer
- Mechanical digger*
- Pegs
- Scissors or a knife
- Shovel
- Skip*
- Soil compactor*
- Spade
- Spirit level
- Straight edge
- String
- Water level*
- Wheelbarrow

? Is it better to buy or hire the tools?

You will probably already have many of the tools if you have a garden, and if you are just starting out you will need to buy some of them anyway. Basic items, such as spades, will be essential garden tools, and most gardeners will also have general tools, such as hammers and spirit levels. The one major item that will need to be hired is a mechanical digger, although if you have a very large garden and are planning a very big pond it might be economical to buy a second-hand one at a farm sale and sell it after you have finished the pond and completed any landscaping you want to do. Most gardeners, however, will find that a small digger, hired with or without an operator, will be more than sufficient. Occasionally you may need to compact the soil, and it is easier to hire a mechanical soil compactor than to do it by hand. The only other tools that you may need to hire are wheelbarrows. Most gardeners have at least one, but if there are several people helping you to get the pond dug, hiring extra barrows will make sense.

Marking out and measuring

? **Is it best to draw up a plan first?**

It is always a good idea to make a plan of what you want to do before you start. You do not have to be an artist: even the roughest sketch and plan will help you visualize what you are trying to do and how you will do it. The building process will be much easier if you can get the pond right the first time round. If the hole is too big it is difficult to replace the earth and compact it sufficiently so that it does not subside, but it is even worse if the levels are wrong and you do not discover this until the pond is filled. Emptying a pond, removing the liner and reconstructing it is not only difficult but demoralizing. If you plan everything as carefully as possible, the whole process will go smoothly. Even write down a list of tools you are likely to require (see pages 30–1) so that everything is at hand when you want it. Do not worry if you cannot draw: this is not a competition and no one else need see it.

? **How do I prepare a plan?**

Start by making an accurate, measured plan of the garden and mark on it all the permanent features, such as trees, borders, lawns and buildings. If you know their position, also draw in the route of any mains services that run across your garden. Then draw the rough outline of the pond you would like. If you are unsure about the position of the pond, take several photocopies of the original garden plan so that you can keep sketching the outline until you find a shape, size and position you like. Alternatively, use tracing paper overlays so that you can assess a number of possible ponds. If possible, make your rough sketches on squared paper so that you can use the grid as a guide when you come to draw out the pond in greater detail to a bigger scale. This step might not be necessary if you are planning a regularly shaped pond, but if the pond is going to have an irregular shape the grid will be useful when you transfer the design to the ground. The plan should include not only the outline of the pond but also an indication of the depths of the pond and where you want planting ledges.

? **How do I transfer the design on the plan to the ground?**

If you do not mind if the finished pond is not exactly as it is shown on the plan, you can mark one or two points on the garden so that its general position is correct and then lay a garden hose on a ground to indicate the desired line. If it is a complicated shape, however, and you want to make sure that it is accurately transferred from your plan, it will be worth replicating the grid on the ground with pegs and strings so that you can carefully place

Marking the pond on the ground

Rather than drawing a plan, you could simply mark the proposed position of the pond on the ground by laying string or a garden hose on the ground. This has the advantage that you can move the outline until you are happy with it. You can also view the proposed pond from different parts of the garden and house, including upstairs windows. Spray paint or sand can also be used (*illustrated above right*), and if you are planning a small pond an old mirror will give you a good indication of how the finished feature will look.

the pipe at the equivalent points on the string where it crosses the grid lines on the plan. Once the pipe is in position, dig around it with a spade or trickle sand from a bottle right round the pipe to mark its position. Remove the pegs, string and pipe and you are ready to start.

? **My garden is sloping. How do I mark it out?**

The pond is laid out in the same way as one on a level plot: work out the outline and then the levels. When you come to construct the pond it will need either cutting into the slope at one end or building up at the other, or, which is more usual, a combination of both. If the pond is going to be a regular shape you will have to take into account the fact that if you mark out the precise shape on the sloping ground, once it is raised to the horizontal (when the banks are formed) the shape will be distorted, and you must allow for this by combining both operations and using the levelling pegs to provide the outline also. When you do this the shape of the pond is

indicated by the tops of the pegs rather than their base. If this sounds confusing, hold a circular lid at an angle and look down on it. Although you know that the lid is circular, because it is at an angle it appears to be oval. The same is happening on the ground. If you mark a precise circle on sloping ground you are, in effect, marking out a shape that will be an oval when the banks are built up to make the sides horizontal.

? **What is the easiest way to mark out a circular pond?**

Place a stake at the point that will be the centre of the pond. Tie a length of string to this. At precisely half the diameter of the pond tie a stick with a sharp point. Walk round in a circle, keeping the string taut and dragging the point of the stick on the ground so that it marks out the circle. Alternatively, tie a bottle filled with dry sand to the string and walk round with this, gently pouring the sand out of the bottle to mark the circumference of the circle. Always keep the string taut.

Excavating the hole

second peg until the top is level with the first. Add another peg farther round the edge of the pond and adjust its height as before. Continue to work around the pond until you are back at the datum peg, which should register as being level with the last peg you have hammered in. The tops of these pegs should form a level platform, and it is from these pegs that you measure and adjust the height of the sides of the pond so that they, too, are level.

? What is the best way to dig a pond?

Start by digging around the perimeter of the pond so that the outline is clearly defined and then restrict all future digging to within this area. Even if you are using a mechanical digger it is safer to mark the outline by hand. First, remove all the topsoil within the outline and place this to one side on a sheet of polythene. Then start on the subsoil, which should be kept separate on another sheet of polythene. Dig the pond down to the depth of the first ledge, keeping the bottom of the excavation level. When you reach the first

? How can I make sure that the top of the pond is level?

Set up a datum peg, which will be your point of reference. The top of this peg marks the level of the top edges of the pond. Hammer another peg into the ground a short distance from the datum peg and rest a spirit level on the tops of both pegs. Adjust the height of the

Levelling the top of the pond

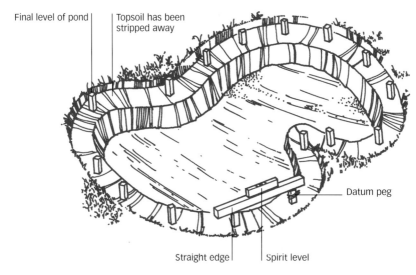

Final level of pond

Topsoil has been stripped away

Datum peg

Straight edge

Spirit level

ledge, mark out the width of the ledge with pegs and draw out the outline of the second ledge. Dig a trench between these outlines and then excavate the soil within it, either down to the level of the next ledge or down to the bottom of the pond, depending on how many ledges you are having.

 What do I do with the spoil?

You will find that an amazing amount of soil comes out of a hole dug for a pond, and there is usually far too much to keep or to lose around the garden. If you keep any of the soil, make sure that it is the topsoil. The subsoil is usually useless from the point of view of the garden and is best discarded. The quickest and easiest but most expensive way of getting rid of it is to hire a refuse skip so that it can be taken away.

If you stack it all in a corner of the garden in the hope that you will have some use for it or that you might find someone who needs it, it could be hanging around for years. There are few uses for the large amount of soil you will get from the pond. A rock garden needs to be free draining, and although topsoil might be suitable, clay subsoils are the last thing you want to include. If part of your garden slopes you may be able to use some of the soil as terracing, but this should be part of your

overall plan from the outset. Topsoil is easier to use and can be spread and mixed with soil on existing borders or used to construct a rock garden, but even this is time-consuming and the best thing may be to get rid of the lot so that you don't have to worry about it.

 What size should I make the hole relative to the size of the finished pond?

The size of the excavated hole will depend on the type of pond you are constructing and the type of liner to be used. The hole for a pond with a geotextile underlay and a flexible liner should be about 1cm (½in) larger than the finished pond, but the difference is so slight that it is usually unnecessary to take it into account. If you are using a preformed liner you will need to make the hole 5–8cm (2–3in) deeper and wider than the liner. If the pond is made of concrete or puddled clay the hole will have to be much larger to accommodate the material. A concrete pond will need at least an additional 10cm (4in) on the depth and on all sides to allow for the thickness of the concrete. A pond made of puddled clay will need a minimum extra 30cm (1ft) all round, 15cm (6in) for the thickness of clay and 15cm (6in) for a layer of soil that will protect the clay and in which plants can grow. If you use bentonite for a puddled pond allow an extra 30cm (1ft) so that a protective layer of soil can be placed on top of the bentonite.

Preformed units

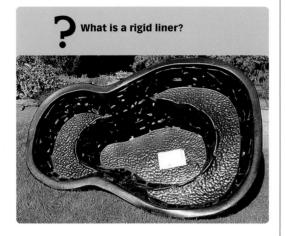

? What is a rigid liner?

although some formal shapes can be found. Preformed pools generally have marginal shelves built into them. Remember: they look larger in the store than they do in the ground.

? How can I dig out the different levels of a rigid preformed liner?

Before you begin marking out and digging, buy the liner so that you can work with the correct dimensions.

The term generally refers to preformed liners, which look a bit like bath tubs. They are usually made of fibreglass, reinforced plastic or some other type of plastic or rubber compound. Fibreglass is the best, and thin, shiny, vacuum-formed plastic shapes are the worst.

Preformed liners are usually suitable for small pools only, and they are available as a complete unit. There is, however, an increasing number of modular units that can be fastened together to make a bigger pool or a series of pools. There are even sections that can be joined together to make streams. Preformed units are usually blue, grey or black and are available in a range of informal shapes,

If the pond is a regular shape simply invert it on the ground and mark around the edges with sand, string or your garden hose. If it is irregular in shape you cannot do this. Instead, you must transfer the shape to the ground while the liner is the right way up, and you will probably need help. Put the liner on the surface of the soil in the exact position that you want the pond to be. If you are working alone, use bricks or building blocks to hold it upright. If you have some canes, insert these at regular intervals of 60–90cm (2–3ft) around the pond, using a spirit level to make sure that the canes are vertical. When the canes are in position, lay string or a hose around them to mark the outline of the liner on the ground (*illustrated below*). Alternatively, using a spirit level or plumb line, drop a series of vertical lines from the edge of the rigid liner to the ground and mark the points on the ground. Go

Shaping the hole for a preformed liner

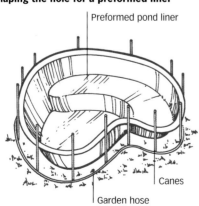

Preformed pond liner

Canes

Garden hose

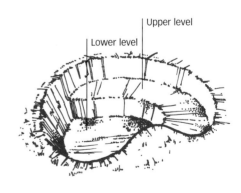

Upper level

Lower level

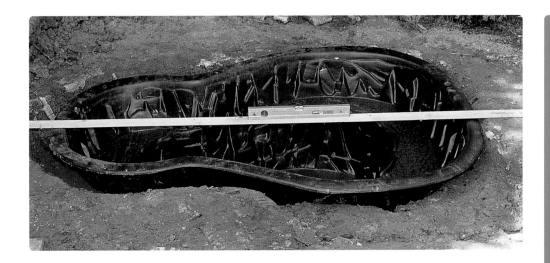

around the liner, dropping verticals at regular intervals, so the outline of the liner is transferred to the ground.

Move the liner out of the way and begin to excavate the hole, working 5–8cm (2–3in) outside the line you have marked. Measure the depth of the first ledge and excavate to about this depth, creating a shallow, level pond. Lightly rake the surface of the soil and place the liner on this in its correct position. Press down the liner to transfer the outline of the deeper zone of the unit to the ground, remove the liner and dig out the next level, again making the hole 5–8cm (2–3in) deeper and wider than the unit.

that the top of the liner is exactly where you want it, which will usually be just beneath the surface of the surrounding soil. When you are satisfied with the height and level of the pond, hold the liner firmly in place and trickle sand down the gap between the soil round the edge of the hole and the liner to a depth of about 10cm (4in). Gently ram it down, taking care not to lift the liner. Add about 10cm (4in) of water to the bottom of the pond and check the levels again. Continue to add sand around the liner and water inside it, checking that the liner is level after each addition. The sand can be further compacted as you go by gently washing it into position with a hose.

? How can I make sure that the top of the preformed liner is horizontal?

When you have excavated the hole for the liner put a 5–8cm (2–3in) layer of soft sand or sifted soil in the base of the hole and stand the pond on it. Place a straight edge across the pool and then put the spirit level on top of this to check that the liner is level both along its length and across its width (*illustrated above*). If the level is not accurate in one or both directions, remove the liner and adjust the level of the sand. At the same time, check

? Does it matter if the liner is not a snug fit in the hole?

Yes; there should be no air pockets around the liner or the sand or soil may wash into them, leaving gaps elsewhere, which may eventually cause the pond to sink in one place or even to crack because it is not properly supported. Bedding the liner firmly in sand or sifted soil is not the easiest of garden jobs, but is worth taking time over the task in order to ensure that there are no air pockets.

Flexible liners

? **What are flexible liners and what are they made of?**

As the name suggests, flexible liners can be bent and folded into shape. When laid in a hole in the ground they mould themselves to all the curves and depressions of the hole and take up its shape (*illustrated below*).

There are several different materials available, varying in cost and lifespan. The cheapest, polythene, has the shortest life, and it is also the most difficult to install, although it is useful for lining bog gardens, where it is buried under soil, well away from ultraviolet light. Butyl rubber is the most expensive but it far outlasts any of the others and so the initial outlay may well be repaid. It is tough, very flexible and its surface is such that it quickly blends into the background and is lost to sight. It also has the advantage of being easy to weld, so odd shapes can be created, and is comparatively easy to repair. In between are

PVC and low-density polythene (LDPE). PVC is the cheaper of the two, but LDPE is easier to lay without wrinkles. They are not as easy as butyl to join or repair. This is really a case of getting what you pay for, with the best results coming from the most expensive materials.

? **How do I calculate how much liner to buy?**

If the pond has vertical sides measure the maximum length of the pond and add to this twice the maximum depth. Add to this 60cm (2ft) to give an overlap at the top of the pond at each end and you have the length required. At right angles to this measure the maximum width, to which you add twice the maximum depth. To this figure again add 60cm (2ft) for overlap and you have the width. The sheet you then require is a rectangle, measuring length × width.

If the sides are sloping make sure you measure the maximum width and length at ground level and not at the base of the pond.

Calculating the size of a liner

When you buy liner for an irregularly shaped pool, calculate the size on the basis of the longest and widest parts of the pond and make sure that you add on twice the depth of the pond and sufficient to give a good overlap all the way round. The following calculation is for an irregularly shaped pool with a maximum length of 4m (13ft), a maximum width of 3m (10ft) and a maximum depth of 60cm (2ft).

Length = length + (2 × maximum depth) + 0.6m (2ft) overlap = 4m (13ft) + 1.2m (4ft) + 0.6m (2ft) = 5.8m (19ft)

Width = width + (2 × maximum depth) + 0.6m (2ft) overlap = 3m (10ft) + 1.2m (4ft) + 0.6m (2ft) = 4.8m (16ft)

Types of flexible liner

	Advantages	Disadvantages
Polythene (polyethylene)	Available in different thicknesses and roll widths; inexpensive.	Only the thickest grade is suitable for lining ponds; quickly deteriorates (hardens and cracks) in ultraviolet light; easily torn; cannot be joined; cannot be repaired; lifespan of only 3–5 years, no guarantees given.
PVC	Available in a range of thicknesses and densities; available in laminated and reinforced types; can be joined; can be repaired; lifespan of 15–20 years; guarantees available according to manufacturer; variable in cost.	Heavy-duty types are difficult to handle and lay.
Low-density polythene (LDPE)	More flexible than standard polythene; difficult to tear; can be repaired; slow to deteriorate in ultraviolet light; lifespan of 15–30 years (depending on finish); guaranteed for 15–30 years; cheaper than butyl.	Cannot be joined.
Butyl	Available in a range of thickness; elasticity makes it stronger and more malleable than other liners; easy to join; easy to repair; resistant to ultraviolet light; lifespan of 50 years or more; usually guaranteed for minimum of 20 years.	Expensive.

Although a pond with sloping sides will need less liner than one with vertical sides, unless the pond is large the difference will not be very great and it is not worth trying to calculate the difference. Inevitably, if the pond is an irregular shape there will some liner left over because it is always purchased as a regularly shaped rectangle. Keep this: it may come in useful for repairs.

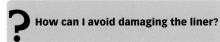

How can I avoid damaging the liner?

First, make sure that you use a good quality underlay between the liner and the underlying soil, the thicker the better. Sharp stones or pieces of wood in the soil can be forced upwards under the weight of the water in the pond, and even though you may have thought you had completely cleared the ground, over time these sharp objects might move upwards and make a hole in the liner above. Make sure, too, that if you place any stones or lumps of concrete in the pool for any reason, these are also separated from the liner by a layer of underlay. Even if they are placed on a layer of soil in the pond they may work their way down to pierce the liner.

Most punctures, however, tend to be caused by people walking or falling in the pond or by someone hitting the liner with a sharp instrument such as a garden fork, so be extra vigilant when you are tending plants in and around the pond.

Using an underlay

Yes; a major problem with all flexible liners is that they are easily punctured. It is impossible to do anything about accidental tears and holes that are caused when you are cleaning the pond or replacing plants, but you can do something about those caused from below. No matter how carefully you excavate the hole, removing stones and plant roots as you go, it is almost impossible to remove every single sharp stone or even pieces of glass, and once the liner is filled with water the weight may force the liner down on to sharp objects.

Lining the surface of the hole with a cushioning, protective material before the liner is laid will protect the liner from the sharpest of stones. It is a false economy to

omit this underlay. Although the soil may seem to be soft and free of stones, there may well be something sharp just below the surface that will be pushed against the liner once the water compresses the loose earth.

Several different materials can be used as underlays. Nowadays the easiest to use and the most reliable are the various non-woven, fabric underlays, known as geotextiles, which are purchased from garden centres or from specialist water centres (*illustrated above*). They are relatively cheap, very tough and easily moulded to shape. Buy the underlay, which is available in rolls of various widths, when you buy the liner.

Geotextiles have all but superseded more traditional materials. Damp builder's sand can be laid in a layer, about 5cm (2in) thick, over all surfaces, including vertical ones. The difficulty arises with vertical surfaces and in corners, because it is essential that the sand is not rubbed off when the liner is installed. The cheapest liner is wads of damp newspapers over the whole surface. Again, the problem is keeping the newspapers in position when you lay the liner. It only needs one section to slip and reveal a stone and the whole project will be jeopardized. In addition, of course, the newspapers will eventually rot away, leaving the liner exposed.

Old carpet underlays can also be used, but they can easily be punctured. Even old carpets can be used, but these are usually not flexible enough to mould around the corners. Although sand, newspapers, carpets and carpet underlays may be cheap or even free, geotextiles are by far the most effective to use.

? How do I get the underlay into position?

If you are using a geotextile, calculate the size required in the same way as for a flexible liner (see pages 38–9). Check the surface of the hole and remove all obvious stones and other objects and then drape the underlay over the bottom of the pond, smoothing it over ridges and into corners. It should continue over the edge of the pool to be buried in the same way as the liner (*illustrated below*) (see pages 42–3).

If you prefer to use sand put a layer about 5cm (2in) deep over the whole prepared surface. The sand should be damp so that it sticks to vertical surfaces and corners. It may be easier to cover these areas with wet newspapers, which can be draped over the edges and down the sides.

Laying a flexible liner

? How do I get the liner into the pond?

Although this is the most exciting stage in building a pond, it is also the most worrying, because if things go wrong it is a lot of work to take it apart and to start again.

First, lay the liner across the pool, stretching it out horizontally for as far as it will go. Drape it loosely over the hole and make sure that it is centred over the pond so that when it sinks into it there will be an equal amount of liner all round the edge. Place paving slabs, bricks or building blocks on the outer edges of the liner. It is a good idea to

Unfolding the liner

If you are building a small pond and have room in the garden, open out the liner and spread it out on the lawn. Leave it to warm up in the sun; this will make it easier to smooth out any creases and make the liner more pliable. If you have ordered a liner for a large pool, follow the manufacturer's instructions about unfolding it. Depending on how the supplier has folded it, the liner may need to be positioned either at one end of the pond or in the centre.

Constructing a pond using a flexible liner

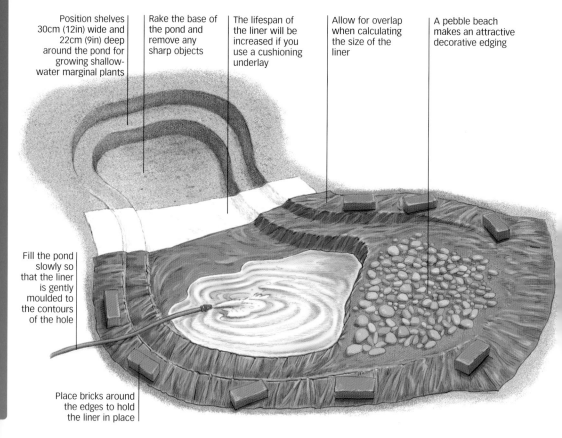

Position shelves 30cm (12in) wide and 22cm (9in) deep around the pond for growing shallow-water marginal plants

Rake the base of the pond and remove any sharp objects

The lifespan of the liner will be increased if you use a cushioning underlay

Allow for overlap when calculating the size of the liner

A pebble beach makes an attractive decorative edging

Fill the pond slowly so that the liner is gently moulded to the contours of the hole

Place bricks around the edges to hold the liner in place

stand these on several thicknesses of newspaper so that any sharp corners do not puncture the liner. The liner will sag slightly over the hole. Place the end of a garden hose in this hollow and begin to fill the liner very slowly. As the hollow fills, the weight of water will drag the liner down into the hole. The stones and bricks should be heavy enough to keep the liner in position so that it is only gradually allowed to sink into the pond. As the liner falls into the pond under the weight of the water, it will mould itself to the shape of the pond. If you are using butyl the liner should sink in smoothly without any creases forming. Other liners are not so easy to use, and you must smooth out any creases that appear. If the liner has been correctly sized and positioned the edges should extend beyond the top edge of the pond by about 30cm (1ft) all round.

? What do I do with the edges of the liner?

The edges of both the underlay and the liner should be buried, and there are a number of ways of doing this. The first is simply to lay the liner over the edge of the pond and along the surface of the soil and then cover this with paving slabs so that it does not show (*illustrated above right*). Alternatively, you can dig a trench about 15cm (6in) away from the edge of the pond. Turn the liner into this and replace the soil. Place slabs over this or cover it with grass. If there is enough liner around the edge of the pond you can create a boggy

margin in which moisture-loving plants will thrive. Dig a trench 60cm (2ft) or more wide to about 30cm (1ft) deep around the pond. Fold the liner into this trench and then up the sides to the surface. Place bricks or stones around the edge of the pond and fill the liner-lined trench behind the stones with soil.

? The edges of the liner can be seen above the water. How can I hide them?

This is a difficult problem to resolve once the pond has been filled with water because it is impossible to straighten out the wrinkles that often make the liner show up.

One solution is to use paving slabs that overhang the edge of the pond and obscure the liner. These must be firmly cemented in place so that they do not tip up when people step on them. An alternative solution is to use plants around the edge of the pond. Choose species that will hang down into the water. Some other edging solutions are described on pages 52–3 and 54–5.

Repairs
Keep any off-cuts that are left over after trimming the liner. They may come in useful if you ever have to repair a puncture or tear in the pond.

Making a bog garden

? **What is the best way to make a bog garden?**

The simplest bog garden is an area of permanently moist soil. Unfortunately, however, just digging humus into the soil will not make the soil sufficiently water retentive to make it into a bog garden. The best method is to dig out a bed, line it with a flexible liner, add a layer of pebbles and gravel and then refill the area with a mixture of soil and well-rotted organic material. Although some bog plants will tolerate stagnant water, most prefer a constantly moist, but not excessively wet, soil around their roots. Therefore, you should puncture the liner with a garden fork so that excess water can drain away. In dry weather the soil can be kept moist by watering with a garden hose from time to time, or you can bury a perforated hose in the soil and attach it to an outside tap, which can be turned on as necessary. Alternatively, a hose pipe can be attached to a water butt that takes rainwater from the house roof and gutters so that it can be directed towards the bog garden.

? **How can I make a bog garden next to my pond?**

It will be easiest if you can construct the bog garden at the same time as the pond. If you

The structure of a bog garden

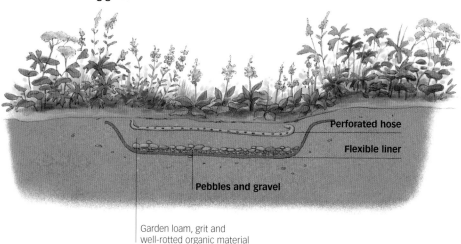

Perforated hose

Flexible liner

Pebbles and gravel

Garden loam, grit and well-rotted organic material

make part of one edge of the pond slightly lower than the rest, when the pond is filled beyond its normal level water will flow over the lower edge into the boggy area next to the pond. The dividing wall or sill between the pond and the bog should be at or just slightly higher than the normal water level in the pond so that it takes only a little extra water, either from excessive rain or when you are topping up the pond with a garden hose, to make it pour over into the bog garden and saturate it. If you want to grow marginal plants – that is, those that normally grow in shallow water – the sill can be a little lower so that the water is permanently just below the surface of the soil.

The construction of the bog garden is the same as described above, except that if you are having a permanently flooded garden for marginals you will not want to puncture holes in the liner.

 Can I put ordinary soil from my garden into the bog garden?

Probably not. The soil in a bog garden should be very moisture retentive and, ideally, neutral to acid. There is no reason why you should not have a bog garden on chalky ground, but it might limit the number of plants you can grow.

Create a moisture-retentive soil by mixing good quality garden loam with equal portions of loam and some form of fibrous material; then mix in one part grit. The fibrous material will help hold the moisture for the plants to

Low-lying ground

If your garden slopes down to an area that is difficult to drain and is always wet, you could turn this into a bog garden. If it is too wet, plant one or two *Salix* spp. (willow), which act as sponges and help to dry out the area.

Soil mix for a bog garden

The soil for a bog garden should be a mixture of good loam and a fibrous material, such as leaf mould or well-rotted compost. It is good idea to add grit to the mixture, because this will make it easier for excess moisture to drain away, while the fibrous material will hold enough moisture for the plants. The proportions are not critical but use roughly 2 parts (by volume) loam, 2 parts fibrous material and 1 part grit.

use, while the grit will allow excess moisture to drain away. A good fibrous material is leaf mould if you have enough in the garden; do not take it from woods, which is environmentally damaging. Very well-rotted garden compost or farmyard manure is a good alternative, although farmyard manure can be too rich unless it is well weathered. Shredded stems of old herbaceous plants and shrubs make an excellent material once they have rotted down. Do not use peat. Not only is its use environmentally unsound but it is also not very good from a gardening point of view because it breaks down rapidly in a bog garden and will constantly need replacing.

Does a bog garden need to be in sun or shade?

If you can, build a bog garden in a sunny position. Although this means that it will dry out more quickly, it will allow you to grow a greater range of plants. Many bog plants, including hostas, can be grown in ordinary garden beds as long as the soil is moist enough, but these plants are usually grown in shade because they cannot get enough moisture in the sun. However, when they are grown in a bog garden there is usually plenty of moisture, and they will happily grow in sun.

Clay ponds

? I want a completely natural pond. What can I use to line it?

Farm ponds and many of the ponds seen in the countryside are usually natural dew ponds (*illustrated right*). These are no more than a hole dug in the ground, often generations ago. If they were dug in pure clay little more was done than to run a flock of sheep through the area of the pond to trample the clay down to make the hole watertight. If the dew pond was dug in a more porous soil or if there were a lot of stones mixed with the soil, a quantity of clay was imported from elsewhere and a layer of clay was placed over the whole pond before being 'puddled' down.

This can still be done, but modern technology has made life much easier for gardeners who want a natural pond. It is possible to buy geotextile blankets or mats that are impregnated with a clay-based substance called bentonite. The matting is laid over the base of the pond, and when it is soaked with water the bentonite expands to form an impermeable barrier. The bentonite can then be covered with a thick layer of soil to help prevent water plants from penetrating it and causing leaks.

Bentonite was originally applied in the form of granules, which were worked into the soil in the bottom and sides of the pond. It can still be purchased in this way, but the impregnated matting is much easier to use and ensures a consistent layer. Do not use bentonite if you have chalky soil.

Digging out a natural pond

When you are excavating the hole for a puddled clay pond make sure that it is deep enough for both the layer of clay and the topping layer of soil, which means allowing at least an additional 30cm (1ft) on all surfaces. Because the clay must be covered with soil, the pond will be more successful if it has gently sloping sides.

? How do I puddle clay?

Before you begin, bear in mind that this is hard work. The traditional approach is to apply a layer of clay, 10–20cm (4–8in) thick, to all the surfaces of an excavated hole. The clay should be wet and pliable and should not have any stones in it.

Work in sections around the pond. If the pond is too big to finish in a single day cover the wet clay with damp sacks or sheets of polythene so that it does not dry out. Apply the clay to the surface and pummel it into place so that it is welded into a solid cover. (If you have children they will have a great time helping.) If you have a large pond, hire a special roller, known as a sheep's foot roller, to help you do the job. Once the clay completely covers the sides and bottom of the pond, cover it with soil to a minimum depth of 10–20cm (4–8in) and then fill the pond with water. Do not let it dry out.

Protecting the clay

To deter burrowing animals and worms from penetrating the clay, it is worth lining the excavated hole with soot before you begin to apply the clay to the pond's base and sides. The clay will also be damaged by questing roots, so water plants with vigorous root systems should be grown in containers. Do not construct a clay pond near to established trees and shrubs and do not plant trees and shrubs near to a clay pond: the roots will penetrate the clay layer and in the course of time they will cause leaks in the pond.

? What shall I do if I do not have clay in my garden?

If you do not have clay in your garden, you may be able to buy it locally. Be careful what you get, however, because you may well be sold a load of clay subsoil that contains roots, stones and other debris, which will make it impossible for you to make a watertight surface. The clay may also be too dry, and you will then have to leave it to dry out completely, break it up into small pieces and then re-wet it until it makes a sticky mass which is suitable for use.

Bentonite granules or matting are a better and easier alternative (*see above*) than traditional clay.

Concrete ponds

? Are ponds still made from concrete?

Although they are not as popular as they once were, ponds are still made from concrete, especially formal ponds, whose regular lines are particularly appropriate for this material.

In the past the choice was between puddled clay and concrete (or a brick or block pond lined with cement or concrete), and most ornamental ponds involved the use of concrete. Now there are rubber and plastic liners that are not only more efficient than concrete in that they do not crack but are also cheaper and easier to install. Nevertheless, there are some situations, formal ponds in particular, where concrete is the preferred material, because it creates a pond with clean, elegant lines and an air of timelessness. The one drawback of modern materials is that nearly all look ugly if they are exposed above the water line, and this is not usually a problem with concrete. In addition, a well-constructed concrete pond should outlast any other material, as long as the ground around it does not move, which can cause cracks (see pages 132–3).

? How thick will the concrete have to be and how much extra should I allow for when I mark out the hole?

The concrete that lines a pond should be at least 10cm (4in) thick. If the pond is on soft soil there should also be a layer of rammed hardcore, blinded with a layer of sand, under the base of the pond and any ledges. This layer should be at least 15cm (6in) thick. On top of this will be the 10cm (4in) layer of concrete. The hole will, therefore, have to be 25cm (10in) deeper and 10cm (4in) wider all round than the finished pond to allow for the hardcore, sand and concrete.

? How can I get an even layer of concrete around the whole pond?

An even depth of concrete is achieved by lining the hole with wooden shuttering (sheets of plywood). The concrete is poured between these and the surrounding soil. As concrete is mainly used for ponds with regular outlines, the shuttering is generally straightforward. First, the hole is lined with polythene to stop soil falling into the hole and mixing with the concrete. The concrete is poured into the base of the pond and allowed to set. Next,

Shuttering for a concrete pond

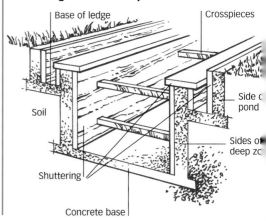

Base of ledge

Crosspieces

Side of pond

Soil

Sides of deep zone

Shuttering

Concrete base

plywood shuttering is built inside the vertical faces 10cm (4in) from the edge of the hole. The shuttering is sprayed with water so that the concrete does not stick, and is held firmly in place by wooden crosspieces placed across the pond. These must be absolutely rigid so that the wood does not move. Pour concrete between the shuttering and the polythene and ram it down so there are no air holes. Wait until it has set and then remove the shuttering. When the concrete is completely set apply a coat of a water-proofing sealant.

Concrete mix

Make your own concrete from the following:
1 part cement, 5 parts aggregate, or
1 part cement, 2 parts sharp sand,
3 parts gravel or small stones

? How do I build ledges in a concrete pond?

The ledges are built in several stages. The base and the lowest section of the side walls are prepared as above, with the shuttering positioned so that the base of the side walls allows for the width of the ledge and the wall. The ledges are laid in the same manner as the bottom. Once these have set, another wall is built above them with new shuttering.

? Should the concrete be reinforced?

If the pond is large or being built on soft ground it is advisable to include reinforcing mesh with the concrete for added strength. Lay half the thickness of the concrete in the base. Place a sheet of reinforced mesh on it and lay the rest of the concrete. The mesh should turn up at the sides so it can be tied to the vertical mesh. Tie in the mesh in the middle of the walls before pouring in the concrete.

For most ponds it will be necessary to reinforce only the corners and the ledges where the pressure will be greatest. Place L-shaped steel rods around the edge of the base concrete so that they stick up into the walls. If there are ledges, place the rods at the junction between the walls and the ledges.

? How do I mix the concrete?

If you are building a large pond it will probably be worth buying ready-mixed concrete. The only drawback is that you must be ready to make the pond when the concrete is delivered because the driver will not wait for you.

Mixing your own allows you to work at your own pace. Mixing by hand is hard work, so think about hiring a cement mixer. You will need a mix of 1 part cement to 5 parts aggregate (which includes sand and stones). Alternatively, if you want to mix your own aggregate, you will need 1 part cement, 2 parts sharp sand and 3 parts gravel. A waterproofing agent can be added to help the pond retain water. Add enough water to make a workable mixture but do not make it runny.

? Is concrete waterproof?

Concrete is reasonably waterproof but not entirely so. The finished surface can be rendered with a thin layer of mortar to which reinforcing fibres have been added. These fibres strengthen the mortar and make it capable of withstanding slight movements in the ground. Alternatively, cover the set concrete with sealant, which not only prevents water penetrating the concrete but also, more importantly, prevents lime and salts leaching out of the concrete into the pool.

Filling and topping up

? When I fill my pond should I use rainwater or tapwater?

Rainwater is by far the best water to use, if for no other reason than it is free of charge. It also is free from chemicals and is usually at the ambient temperature. Tapwater contains chlorine and fluorine as well as other chemicals to make it safe for humans to drink. It is also often very cold, especially if it has come from underground. Adding just a small amount of tapwater to the pond to top it up in very hot weather should not be a problem, but if you completely fill a pond with mains water let it stand for several days before introducing plants and wildlife so that there is time for the chemicals to disperse and the temperature to rise.

? How can I make sure the water level is kept topped up?

The best way of keeping the pond topped up is to run excess water from house and shed roofs into the pond. This may involve some disruption to the garden so that the necessary pipes can be laid, but it will save a lot of time and effort in the long run and, if your water is metered, it will save you money. The alternative is to use a garden hose from the nearest tap.

With some ponds, especially those with fountains, where water may be blown out of the pond altogether or evaporates quickly, it may be necessary to have a connection to the mains supply. This does not mean that water runs constantly from a tap into the pond; instead, there is a ball valve in a reservoir, similar to a lavatory cistern, so that the water is turned on when the water in the pond drops below a certain level. It would be necessary to install non-return valves, so this is probably a job for a qualified plumber, and you might also have to get permission from the local water authority.

? What happens to excess water?

If the pond is usually topped up with a garden hose from the mains water supply then it is unlikely that the pond will ever become over-full. The normal water level will be several

A pond with a soakaway

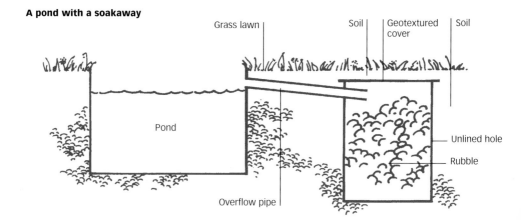

Grass lawn | Soil | Geotextured cover | Soil

Pond

Unlined hole

Rubble

Overflow pipe

centimetres (1–2in) below the level of the top edge, and any rainwater can normally be easily accommodated. If, however, the water supply is taken from roofs and other hard surfaces at times of heavy rainfall, the pond may overflow. Some gardeners ignore this problem and let the water filter away through the surrounding soil. However, it is possible to take a more practical approach and build an overflow pipe, which takes away excess

water. This may go to a nearby ditch or drainage channel or it may be directed into a soakaway.

A soakaway is a hole, usually about 1m (3ft) in all directions, which is filled with clean rubble. It is covered with a piece of geotextile, which is topped with a layer of soil so that once built it is never seen. Water flows from the pond into this and gradually soaks away into the surrounding soil.

can be edged with paving stones as a contrast. If the pond is raised above ground level, the edge is often most appropriately created by large paving stones, which not only hide the liner and the construction of the walls but also provide a convenient place to sit.

? How can I build a solid edge around my pond?

The simplest form of hard edging to a pond is paving slabs (*illustrated left*). If the pond is in the middle of your patio this will be the obvious solution, anyway, but it will also work in other areas, including gravel gardens or even when the pond is set in grass. It is possible to make or buy slabs that are slightly tapered so that they fit snugly together around curves, but you can use square ones if you add a fillet of cement between them to take up the curve. It is essential that the slabs are firmly fixed, and they are best secured by bedding them down in cement or concrete. The concrete should be laid over the edge of the liner in a smooth layer and the slabs are laid on the bed of mortar. Add or remove concrete as necessary to make sure that the slabs are even.

Paved edgings

? I have a formal garden. How should I edge my pond?

If the surface of the pond is at ground level and is set within a gravelled area, you will need to use paving stones or bricks to edge the pond (*illustrated right*), both to disguise the edge of the liner and to stop gravel constantly falling into the pond. If it is set at ground level within a paved or brick area, laying paving stones or bricks right up to and slightly over the edge of the water will hide the liner. For safety's sake it is often a good idea to highlight the pond by using a different material, colour or shape of paving around the edge. If, for example, it is set in a brick patio the bricks round the pond could be set on edge to contrast with the flat-laid bricks, or it can it

Solid edging a pond

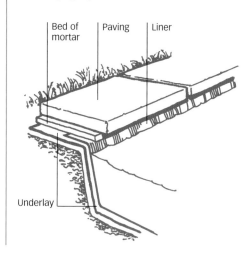

Bed of mortar | Paving | Liner

Underlay

? **The paving slabs are slumping towards the pond. What has gone wrong?**

This could have happened simply because the slabs were not laid properly and have come loose. First lift all the slabs from around the pond. Next excavate a shallow trench right round the pond, and fill this trench with concrete to make a firm and stable base. Make sure that the edges of the pond liner are under the concrete.

Bed the slabs down on to the concrete base, making sure that they are level or have just the slightest of slopes towards the pond so that rainwater is shed into it.

It is more serious if the paving slabs are not level because the edge of the pond was not properly constructed and the ground is giving way or the whole of the bank is slowly falling into the pond. Whatever the cause, you will have to rebuild the bank. This may mean emptying the pond completely so that you can reinforce the sides. Again, lay the slabs on a solid base of concrete.

Safety first
Any paving around the edge of the pond must be firmly bedded in concrete. If it rocks or is uneven people may trip and fall into the water. Children will love to run around the pond and could easily trip on unsteady or uneven surfaces and possibly fall in.

Edging with lawns and borders

? Can I surround an informal pond with grass or can I use other land-based beds?

Informal ponds can be surrounded by grass, but they are likely to look like an oasis stuck out in isolation. It is better to integrate them into the wider garden. Planting borders near the pond helps, especially if they lead to the water's edge. A bog garden would be ideal, but it could be an ordinary border with plants, such as astilbes and rodgersias, that go well with water. For a wildlife pond rough grass would be better than a close-mown lawn.

? What kind of edging is appropriate for an informal pool?

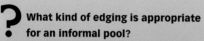

Plants make excellent edging for this type of pool because they tend to blur the margins. They also provide secrecy and cover for wildlife visiting the pool. Plants should not completely surround the pond, however. Leave at least some of the bank showing so

Grass edges

One of the problems with edging a pond with grass is to stop the grass eventually growing into the water, where it will be out of reach of the mower. A length of timber as an edge between the water and the grass will stop the grass growing into the water, and if you make sure that the top of the timber is below the level of the grass, you will be able to mow up to the water's edge. Another problem is that if the grass is subject to heavy wear the ground underneath may crumble. One solution is to mortar in bricks or blocks to make a solid edge to the pool outside the liner. If the blocks are about 3–5cm (1–2in) below the grass, it will be able to grow down to the water's edge but the ground will not crumble.

that the water is visible. Here grass is often the best for of edging, although if it slopes towards the water it can be difficult to mow.

A path of paving or gravel can just touch the pond, but for an informal pond it should not go right round as this gives a formal feel. Where there are no plants a feature can be made of supporting the bank with logs – making an attractive informal edge.

? I want to build a natural pond. How can I create a natural-looking sloping shore into it?

When excavating the pond make sure that at least one section of the bank has a very gentle slope; because this takes a fair amount of room you will need a pond of a reasonable size. It is possible to create a gentle slope in a small pond if the pond is shallow.

Build the pond in the usual way, laying an underlay and then a liner. If you wish, lay a further layer of geotextile underlay on top of the liner. Arrange a layer of graded cobbles and pebbles on the slope, positioning them so that they run from above the water line on the dry shore into the water until they disappear into the gloom or waterweeds. To stop the cobbles sliding down the slope into the water, mortar a low retaining wall of larger pebbles around the pond below water level. An alternative would be to cover this area with sand, but this would quite quickly become filled with soil.

Dry land

Remember that unless you have actually created a special boggy area, the soil around the pond is usually dry and not moist as one would imagine. This is because the liner, whether it is preformed or butyl, will, as intended, keep the water in the pond and not allow it to seep into the surrounding soil. If you want to grow water-associated plants close to the pond you may have to create a special moist or boggy bed for them.

? Can I build a flower border right up to the edge of the pond?

You can take beds right up to the edge of your pond as long as you haven't run the liner of the pond over the edge of the bank and buried it horizontally, which will impede planting. Instead, make sure that the liner is buried vertically. In an informal pond the beds not only run up to the edge of the pond but the planting often continues beyond it and into the water. The plants immediately next to the pond tend to look best if they are ones that naturally grow near to water, although most garden plants will do. It is better to avoid having bedding plants and bedding schemes too close to a pond; these associate better with dry areas.

Making a cobble beach

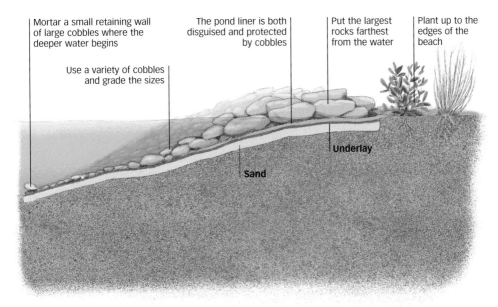

Mortar a small retaining wall of large cobbles where the deeper water begins

Use a variety of cobbles and grade the sizes

The pond liner is both disguised and protected by cobbles

Put the largest rocks farthest from the water

Plant up to the edges of the beach

Underlay

Sand

Free-standing containers

? Can I use a half-barrel as a pond?

As long as it is watertight, a half-barrel will make an attractive small pond. Half-barrels are often sold in garden centres as planters, and you might find one that will not leak. If you can, choose one that has been standing outdoors, because the timber will be wet and will not have shrunk.

Another sign that the timbers have not dried out is if the metal hoops are still firmly in position around the outside of the barrel. Wash the barrel thoroughly, leave the timbers to dry and then paint the interior with a silicone sealant. Leave this to dry, then apply a coat of black pool waterproofing paint. Wait

for a day or two before filling the half-barrel with water. If you prefer, use a small piece of flexible liner to line the half-barrel. Hold the liner in position with battens and pins above the water line.

? Can I turn any container into a pond?

There really is no limit to what you can use, although if it is going to be positioned above ground it should be visually acceptable. Half-barrels and galvanized containers, such as old baths and even buckets, are among the most popular.

Old porcelain or galvanized sinks and troughs are also very popular and are ideal for use with waterspouts or small waterfalls. Odd containers can also be used – galvanized dustbin lids and even old car hub caps can be used to make shallow ponds.

Keeping fish in a small pond

There is no reason you should not keep two or three fish in a container as small as a half-barrel, provided you bear in mind the general rule about stocking levels: 5cm (2in) of fish for every 30 × 30cm (1 × 1ft) of water surface. Unless the container is sunk into the ground, however, the water temperature will fluctuate widely, becoming too hot in summer and freezing readily in winter. Try to position the container in a sheltered position on your patio, with perhaps another container in front of it to protect it from very hot sun and very cold winds.

If you are going to sink the container into the ground you can use anything at all, although containers with white interiors are not ideal. Small aluminium or galvanized containers can be sunk into the ground to form a pattern, and you can even use tins, although they will quickly rust.

? **I have an old white kitchen sink. What's the best way to use it as a pond?**

Old sinks are very heavy, so make sure it is in position before you fill it with water. If liked, they can be covered with a material called hypertufa, which can be mixed from 1 part sharp sand, 1 part cement and 2 parts sphagnum peat (or peat substitute). Add sufficient water to make a stiff mixture. Use a pan scourer to abrade the surface of the sink; this will make it easier to get the hypertufa to stick to it. Cover the surface of the sink with industrial glue and cover this with hypertufa. Remember to cover the top edge. Leave the hypertufa to dry for several days, and protect it from strong sunlight, which might crack the surface. Put a plug into the drainage hole and seal it with waterproof silicone sealant. Paint the surface with milk, yogurt or a proprietary antiquing fluid to make it darken more quickly.

3 Other Water Features

Kits and accessories

? **I would like a small, self-contained water feature. What alternatives to pebble fountains are there?**

It is possible to buy kits for small Japanese-style water features, and these are appropriate in gardens with restrained, minimalist planting, such as grasses, irises

and small bamboos. The feature known as a *shishi odoshi*, deer scarer, consists of a reservoir, which is buried underground. A submersible pump raises the water through a vertical bamboo post, from where it flows into a narrower piece of bamboo.

The water runs into a large, partially hollowed out piece of bamboo, which is arranged so that it pivots. When the large piece of bamboo is full of water, it tips forward on its pivot, and spills the water into the reservoir below, which is hidden by gravel and carefully arranged cobbles. It is called a deer scarer because the large piece of bamboo is balanced in such a way that it swings backwards and strikes a large rock when the water has emptied out of it into the reservoir beneath.

Also available in kit form is another simple Japanese-style water feature, the *tsukubai*, which has a container that is constantly filled with water from a bamboo stem. The water spills over gravel or stones into a hidden reservoir beneath to be recirculated by a submersible pump (*illustrated left*).

? Do all water features need to be connected to an electricity supply?

An increasing range of solar-powered water features is becoming available, and the style of these is improving all the time. One drawback is that most need a solar panel, which has to be positioned in a sunny site. Pumps that will circulate up to 400 litres (90 gallons) of water can be operated from solar panels, although these are fairly obtrusive and have to be sited close to the pond.

Small fountains, giving a spray about 60cm (2ft) high, are available with integral solar panels, and these are capable of circulating up to 100 litres (25 gallons) of water. Floating solar lights, also with integral panels, will give 6–8 hours of light at night; the disadvantage is that they cannot be turned off at will.

The general advantages of solar-powered accessories are that they are safe to use, easy to install and cost nothing to run.

? Can I have a water feature on my balcony?

Yes; several small water features are available that can be easily accommodated on a balcony or the corner of a small patio. It is possible to buy kits with ceramic containers, submersible pumps and different arrangements of decorative pebbles.

You can even get kits with various arrangements of leaf shapes (usually made of copper), over which water trickles down to a container, to be recirculated to the top leaf or more elaborate designs that you can use to make illusions (*illustrated above*). These small features take up little space but provide the refreshing sound of trickling water and a moist atmosphere for plants such as ferns and hostas.

Make sure, however, that your balcony can support the weight of the water feature you are planning. If you are unsure, get a surveyor to advise you.

Pumps and filtration systems

How do I install a pump for a fountain?

Modern submersible pumps are easy to set up. So that the inlet of the pump does not get clogged up with debris and sediment on the bottom of the pond, you generally need to stand the pump on blocks or bricks placed in the base of the pond; if your pond has a flexible liner, stand the blocks on off-cuts of underlay to protect the liner from accidental damage. In a deep pond the pump and spray unit may need to be raised on even more bricks or blocks so that the nozzle is just above the water's surface. If you do not want a pump that is visible below the surface of the water, it is possible to get a surface pump, which can be installed above water level on dry land with a pipe running to a vertical tube and nozzle in the centre of the pond.

Fortunately, most modern pumps are supplied with electric cables already attached to them. This is important because the connection must be waterproof so that your work begins once the cable is safely on dry land. However, it is better to get a qualified electrician to connect it to a power supply. Cover the emerging cable with a rock so that it cannot be seen. This is better than running it through the side of the pond, as this may be difficult to seal properly. Although you can use overhanging plants to disguise the cable, this is not advisable as it is all too easy to forget that it is there and to sever it when you are cutting back the plants.

How do I install a pump for a stream?

The water in a stream is drawn from the bottom pool and pumped to the top of the run, where it can enter the stream in a variety of ways. It can, for example, trickle from under a stone in the manner of a spring, or it can well up in another pool so that the water pours over a lip into the stream. If you prefer it can come over a cascade or even emerge from a waterspout or fountain.

Cross-section along stream

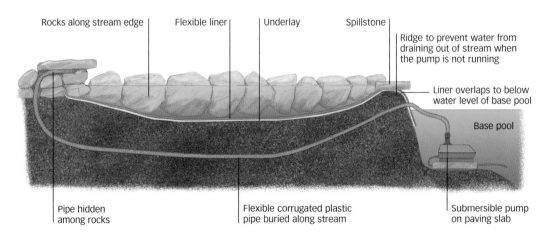

Rocks along stream edge | Flexible liner | Underlay | Spillstone |

Ridge to prevent water from draining out of stream when the pump is not running

Liner overlaps to below water level of base pool

Base pool

Pipe hidden among rocks

Flexible corrugated plastic pipe buried along stream

Submersible pump on paving slab

If you use a submersible pump place it in the bottom pool and run the outlet pipe (and the electricity cable) out of the pool, hiding them with a rock or two. (This is easier than trying to take it through the side of the pool and make a watertight exit point.) The pipe runs alongside the stream, up to the top pool. If possible, bury the pipe under rocks so that it will not be disturbed when you are digging and weeding.

Do I need a filtration system in my pond?

If you have a small water feature with a hidden or partially concealed reservoir of water and no plants (*illustrated above right*), you will not need a filtration system. A large, well-balanced pool is unlikely to need a filter, but if you keep a lot of fish or have a shallow pond in which the water warms quickly on sunny days, you might want to consider a filter.

There are two types of pond filters. Biological filters need a pump that will run continually, especially in summer, and if you live in an area of mild winters it might have to be run in winter, too. They operate by turning harmful nitrites into beneficial nitrates. Water passes through a filter medium (clay, carbon granules and so on) on which beneficial bacteria flourish; these bacteria break down the harmful waste products and gases. Mechanical filters can be run intermittently. The water is sucked through the filter medium, and debris is removed before the water is discharged through the pump unit.

Ultraviolet clarifers can be used with biological filters. They expose the water to ultraviolet light, which makes the algae bunch together, so they are easier to collect.

Buying a pump

It will make your life easier if you have worked out the answers to the following questions when you go to buy a pump from a garden centre or specialist aquatic centre:

- What do you want to use the pump for – that is, what sort of fountain or watercourse will it be powering?
- What are the approximate measurements of your pond?
- If you want a fountain, how high will the spray be and what style of spray do you want?

- If you are building a watercourse, how long and how wide will the stream be?
- If you are creating a stream, will the water trickle gently or would you like faster-moving water that will gush over a waterfall or a series of waterfalls?
- Will you want a pump that runs all the time or intermittently?
- Will the pump be fitted in a pond in which there are fish? If so, do you need a biological filter to keep the water clear?

Features with recirculated water

? **Are there any water features that do not have open water?**

There are several types of water feature that do not involve open water. Such features are eminently suitable for small gardens and patios as they are usually quite small in size. They are also perfect for gardens in which young children play as there is no standing water as a possible safety hazard. These water features have in common a reservoir of water, which is usually hidden below ground and covered by a strong metal grid.

Spread across the grid are decorative pebbles or rocks on which water splashes, either from a bubble jet from below or from a waterspout above.

The water hits the rocks and immediately disappears between them into the reservoir below, from which it is pumped up again, via the spout or jet. This provides the sound and glint of water but is virtually risk free.

? **Can I put a millstone fountain on my patio?**

If you have a suitable electric connection, small water features such as millstone fountains are ideal for patios, but consider if you will be able to house the reservoir – these features rarely look satisfactory if they are raised too high above ground level. If you can lift one or more of the paving stones so that you can excavate a hole to accommodate the reservoir, which will be at least 30cm (1ft) deep and about 60cm (2ft) across, a millstone feature will be an attractive addition to a patio and would be a delightful addition to a planting of shade- and moisture-loving plants.

? **Can I use a terracotta container with a submersible pump?**

Yes; brimming urn fountains are a good alternative to pebble and millstone features if you want a feature with height but do not want large areas of water. These features are also safer for children than traditional ponds.

Brimming urn

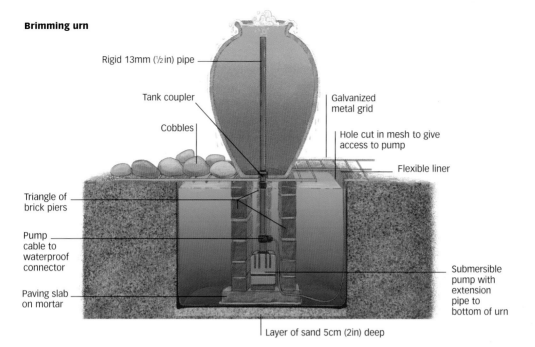

Rigid 13mm (½ in) pipe

Tank coupler

Cobbles

Galvanized metal grid

Hole cut in mesh to give access to pump

Flexible liner

Triangle of brick piers

Pump cable to waterproof connector

Submersible pump with extension pipe to bottom of urn

Paving slab on mortar

Layer of sand 5cm (2in) deep

The increased popularity of this type of feature has meant that it is now possible to buy urns in various styles, colours and sizes with holes predrilled in the base to accommodate the pipe from the pump. The fountains are constructed in the same way as a millstone fountain, with an underground reservoir that contains a submersible pump. The water pipe passes through the hole in the bottom of the urn. The pump forces water up through the pipe and the excess trickles gently over the sides of the urn to return to the reservoir below. The urn stands on a grid, in the same way as the cobbles or millstone, and the area around the base of the urn can be hidden with graded cobbles or gravel. If you use a large urn, you will need to build special piers of mortared bricks to support the urn, which will be too heavy when full of water for the metal grid alone.

Topping up

When small water features such as millstone, cobble and brimming urn fountains are run for long periods in hot, sunny weather, it is important to make sure that the reservoir is kept topped up with water so that it does not evaporate away. Operating these fountains when there is insufficient water in the reservoir will damage the pump.

Wall-mounted features and waterspouts

A waterspout is a single-jetted spout, much like that on a drinking fountain. Normally it will spout from a tube in a wall or be supported on a column. The spout is often surrounded by a piece of sculpture or an animal mask: lions' heads are a particularly popular design. The water trickles in a continuous stream, arching down into a pool of some kind. This may not be a conventional pool; it could be a trough or sink. If the container is not big enough to house a hidden pump, a reservoir is buried beneath the trough. The water trickles from the top of the trough down into the reservoir, and it is from here that the water is pumped back up to the spout.

Unusual spouts

An old hand pump with a stream of water emerging from the nozzle would make an unusual but appropriate water feature. The water falls on to a iron grid and disappears into a hidden reservoir, from which it is pumped back up and out of the hand pump.

? **Do I need a pond for a waterspout?**

No; waterspouts are ideal for small gardens, especially courtyard gardens, because they can be used without a pond. Water pours into a container of some kind, often a trough, but it could be a bucket or old bath if that would not look out of place in your garden. The amount of open water could be further reduced by having the water pour over a group of cobbles or large pebbles, through which it drains into a hidden reservoir below.

? **Can I attach a waterspout to a house wall?**

No; no matter how carefully you prepare the surface behind the waterspout the wall will absorb some water. These attractive features really need the construction of a false wall or double wall so that the delivery pipe from the pump to the wall spout is hidden. If there is an existing, free-standing wall with a

Installing a wall fountain

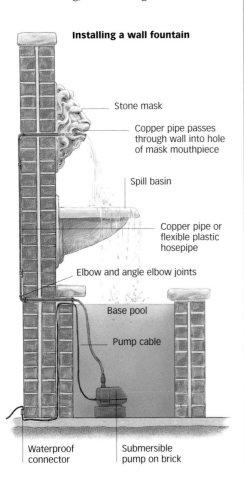

Stone mask

Copper pipe passes through wall into hole of mask mouthpiece

Spill basin

Copper pipe or flexible plastic hosepipe

Elbow and angle elbow joints

Base pool

Pump cable

Waterproof connector

Submersible pump on brick

suitable cavity, the hose can be pulled through this, although you will have to make entry and exit holes.

? **Can I have a wall-mounted waterspout in my courtyard garden?**

If you can find a satisfactory way to hide the pipework and if you have space for a hidden reservoir or a trough to act as a reservoir, there is nothing to stop you having such a fountain on any but the house wall. An ideal way to disguise the pipework is trellis, which can be fixed 2.5cm (1in) away from the wall on battens. This will support the mask, give space for the pipe and allow climbing plants to grow and hide the pipe. To protect the wall, apply a proprietary water sealant. If you can dig a hole in the ground in front of the wall, use a plastic dustbin as a reservoir. Stand it on a bed of soft sand with its rim slightly below ground level. Alternatively, use a trough as a reservoir or build a raised pool. Position a submersible pump in the bottom of the reservoir. Pass a copper pipe through the hole in the mask and attach one end to of a length of corrugated flexible hose with a hose clip. Pass the hose behind the trellis and into the reservoir. Attach it to the pump outlet and fill the reservoir with water. Cover the top of the dustbin with a metal grid and cobbles.

Fountains

? **Is it essential to have a fountain in a pond?**

No; in fact, most ponds do not have fountains. However, the effect of a fountain is extremely attractive, as the water sparkles in sunlight, and the sound that the water generates can be very pleasant. From the practical point of view, a fountain will help to introduce air into the water, especially in summer and in hot, thundery weather, preventing it from becoming stagnant, and if you have fish this can be an important consideration.

? **Can I put a fountain in any sort of pond?**

Some gardeners prefer not to put fountains in informal and wildlife ponds, simply because most of the fountains that are available in aquatic suppliers look too formal for such a setting, but if you use your imagination you could create a fountain from, say, a group of vertical bamboo tubes, which would certainly fit in with the style of your pond and be a pleasant surprise to visitors to your garden.

In most gardens fountains are most appropriate in formal ponds. They are generally placed in the centre of a square or round pond, but in a rectangular pond it might be more interesting to use two fountains, one at each end. Although it is possible to buy all manner of complicated spray formations, the simplest styles are often the most successful. Don't forget when you are building the pond that you will need to get electricity to the pond in the most unobtrusive way possible and to plan for it at an early stage.

? **How high should the fountain be?**

The height of the spray will depend on the size of your pond. In general, the height of the fountain should not be greater than the

Styles of fountain jet

Many styles of fountain jet are available, from single spouts to multiple sprays. If you have space, you could have a bell-shaped jet, a tiered arrangement, a plume of water, a geyser or a surface jet. The outlet can range from a simple nozzle to fanciful ornaments in the form of cherubs, fish, birds, dolphins or even humans.

Installing a fountain

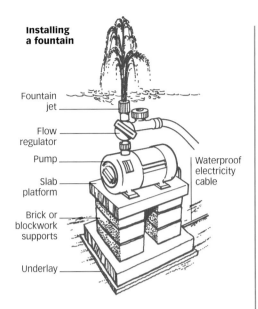

Fountain jet

Flow regulator

Pump

Slab platform

Brick or blockwork supports

Underlay

Waterproof electricity cable

diameter of the pond. A wide spray, which is broken by several fine jets of different heights, will need a clear, wide pond to catch the spray so that the fountain does not lose too much water in windy weather. Remember, too, that your neighbours may not appreciate the spray from your fountain being blown into their garden. When you buy a pump you should know the height and spread of the fountain you want to install so that you buy the appropriate model.

? Do I have to leave the fountain on all the time?

No; you can switch on the pump whenever you want to. If you wish, you can run it during the day or, if the pond is lit, in the evening and switch it off at night.

It is certainly best to turn fountains off during cold weather when they are likely to freeze. Although the resulting ice can look extremely beautiful, it is likely to damage the pump. It is possible to get 'magic eyes' that operate in much the same way as some security lights and will switch on the fountain as a person approaches.

? Can I have a fountain without a pump?

Fountains were used before submersible pumps were available, of course, but you would need a reservoir of water above the point where you want the fountain. If you have a natural head of water, the pressure of the water will force it into the air in the same way as the tank in your roof space creates pressure in your taps. If you live in hilly country you may be able to have a pump-free fountain, but otherwise you will have to use a solar-powered fountain or fit an electric cable.

? Can I use a fountain in a wildlife pond?

Although fountains look out of place in wildlife ponds, which are designed to be as natural as possible, some birds love to bathe under them. If you have a simple fountain in your pond, stand a rock in the water under the spray so that the birds have something to perch on. A more natural alternative would be to have a waterfall.

Streams and waterfalls

The widespread availability of small pumps, which recirculate water, means that you can have a stream in almost any type of garden. You will need to create a channel down which the water will circulate, and this can be made from strips of flexible liner, preformed stream sections or concrete. Flexible liner is the most versatile, but preformed units are available with matching header and bottom pools.

The main problem is recirculating the water back to the beginning. This is usually achieved by allowing the stream to trickle into a pool from which a pump sends the water back up to the top where it re-emerges as a 'spring', spout or simple overflowing pool.

? **Can I have a stream in a flat garden?**

It is possible to have a completely flat stream because the flow is created by water falling into a pool at one end, thereby raising the water level so it runs into a reservoir, but it will be more successful if there is at least a slight slope, to give a more active flow. For many gardeners the most interesting streams are those down a quite steep slope that provide the sound of tumbling water, more like a mountain stream than a meandering brook, and the traditional way of achieving this is to build a large rock garden and have the stream running down this, perhaps broken by occasional pools on the way down.

? **How do I build a stream?**

First, work out where it is going to go. It is important that it is integrated into the rest of the garden, especially if it is going to be of any length. Any slopes, such as rock gardens, that the water will pass down should be built and the bed of the stream thoroughly compacted. Do not get over-ambitious and try to create a huge waterway because the amount of water that can be pumped will depend on the capacity of your pump, and most of the pumps sold for ordinary garden use will not be powerful enough to move more than about 2,700 litres (600 gallons) an hour.

Excavate the waterway and line it with underlay in the same way as you would a pond. Lay the strips of flexible liner along the length of the stream, starting from the bottom and moving upwards. Butyl is best because you can weld the strips together where they overlap. Bury the sides of the underlay in the banks of the stream or turn it in a sharp inverted U so that the liner goes over the bank and then vertically into the soil. You do not want it to run too far horizontally or it will be difficult to plant the banks. Depending on the type of liner used, weld or tape the joints so that they are waterproof. At the bottom of the run create a stone ledge over which the water pours into a small pool.

The pipe that returns the water from the bottom pool (where the submersible pump is placed) to the header pool should be buried in the ground along the edge of the stream.

? **What are the best plants to grow along the stream?**

The type of planting along the stream will depend on the type of garden you have, but most streams look best with plenty of greenery, such as hostas and ferns, brightened with flowers such as primulas for spring and summer and mimulus (musk) for summer and autumn. Most of the plants that are grown as marginals can be used (see pages 88–9), but avoid using ordinary garden plants, such as bedding plants – *Impatiens* (busy lizzies), for example – and roses, because they will look out of place. If you have a large garden, plants such as *Gunnera*

manicata (giant rhubarb) will look dramatic. Plant in groups and leave one or two stretches of the bank bare, with perhaps grass or rocks, or even paving.

? **Is it difficult to build a waterfall?**

No; all you need are two pools, one higher than the other. Part of the edge of the upper pool is lowered so that water can flow from it, over a lip, down into the lower pool. You can arrange a slab of rock or large stone across the lip, which will give the effect of a sheet of water, or you can arrange several rocks to break up the water as it falls. A pump in the lower pool returns water to the top.

A cascade can be made in a similar way by connecting two pools with a steep rocky stream, creating a series of small pools and tumbling water. In a modern garden you can create a curtain of water falling down a vertical slab of rock into a narrow pool below. The position of the upper pool can be so high that it cannot to be seen: the water just pours over the edge of the slab above eye level.

Stream-side plants

The following will look appropriate planted near a stream:

- *Astilbe* x *arendsii*
- *Dryopteris erythrosora* (copper shield fern)
- *Gunnera manicata* (giant rhubarb)
- *Hosta* cvs. (pictured right)
- *Iris ensata* (syn. *I. kaempferi*)
- *Lythrum* spp. (loosestrife)
- *Mimulus lewisii* (great purple monkey flower)
- *Primula denticulata* (drumstick primrose)
- *Rodgersia podophylla*
- *Trollius cultorum* cvs. (globeflower)

Decking

? What is decking?

Decking is basically little more than a wooden platform. It has become a popular alternative to paving in many gardens, and can be used to create an area where you can walk, sit and entertain. In many ways it resembles an indoor wooden floor, with a frame on which planks or strips of wood are nailed. The deck can be at ground level or raised. On sloping ground it may even extend out through the tops of trees or shrubs planted lower down. The same idea is often used for ponds, where the deck can be built out across the water.

? Can I use decking near my pond?

Decking is an extremely sympathetic material to use near a pond. Although it is a linear, strongly defined surface, it even works well

with informal ponds, although care is needed so that it does not dominate the pond.

You can use decking in one of two main ways. The first is simply to have the decking running beside the pond, perhaps as a substitute for paving. This kind of decking is relatively easy to build because it is entirely on firm ground. The alternative is to start on firm land and project the decking out over the water. Usually, the decking would be only a few centimetres (1–2in) above the water, but it could be much higher if, for example, the decking extended from your patio over a pond in the garden below. There is something soothing in being able to sit or stand out above water, perhaps watching fish or other

Laying decking

Decking can be laid in various geometrical patterns, but you may have to set the bearers closer together for complex herringbone or checkerboard arrangements than is necessary for straightforward planking.

activity in the water below. Decking that projects at least a little way beyond the margin of the pond has the additional advantage of masking the edge of the liner.

? What wood should I use for decking?

Although decking can be made from almost any kind of timber, always use pressure-treated or tanalized timber that is 2.5cm (1in) thick. Hardwood is best because it will last longer and will be less inclined to produce splinters. There are several suitable hardwoods, including beech, mahogany and oak, but they are likely to be relatively expensive. Softwood is much cheaper but must be planed and treated with preservative. Softwoods are derived from coniferous trees, such as larch and pine.

You can use planks or tiles. Planks are 15–20cm (6–8in) wide and is supplied in lengths of 3–4m (10–13ft). Tiles are usually 45cm (18in) square. For safety, use decking planks and tiles that have a ribbed or grooved surface to prevent slipping.

? How do I lay decking?

If the decked area is on firm ground, clear the ground of weeds and rake it level. The planks or tiles rest on joists or bearers, which are normally made of 8 × 5cm (3 × 2in) tanalized timber. The bearers themselves should be positioned on special pads, which are made of precast concrete and are about 45cm (18in) square and 10cm (4in) thick. The pads are set on the ground so that they are about 1.2m (4ft) apart. The bearers sit firmly in grooves in the tops of the pads and are positioned so that they run at right angles to the decking planks. The bearers run parallel to each other, about 75cm (30in) apart. The decking planks

are screwed to the bearers; leave a gap of 5–10mm (¼–½in) between each plank to allow for expansion and drainage. All fixings should be of galvanized steel or some other rust-proof material.

Building out across a lined pond is more difficult, but the principle is the same. The soil under the liner must be firm so that it will not subside. Lay pads of geotextile on the liner and build large concrete blocks with vertical supports sunk into them; the frames and deck are built on to these supports.

? What is the best way of maintaining the condition and colour of the decking?

Wood changes colour as it weathers, and this is part of its attraction. However, to keep it in good condition the decking should be treated with one of the many products on the market. Some will help restore the original colour, while others will stain it, either in an imitation wood colour or an artificial one. The wood should be dry before you begin work: rub down the surface with a wire brush or sandpaper to remove any lichen or dirt. All decking should be treated with preservative from time to time to prevent it from rotting. Sometimes the colouring agent and the preservative are combined. Some preservatives, creosote, for example, should not be used because they harm plants and fish, so check the suitability of any product.

Bridges and stepping stones

? Is it worth building a bridge across a small pond?

A large bridge over a small pond will look out of scale and probably rather silly, but one or two stone slabs, with no dominant handrails, positioned over a narrow strip of water would be appropriate. Normally, however, put bridges where they look as if they are fulfilling a function. You can walk round a small pond, so a bridge would be redundant, but if your have a long pond or a stream a bridge will have a purpose and will not look out of place.

? What is the best material for a bridge?

Bridges can be built from just about any waterproof material. Brick, stone, painted iron and tanalized wood can all be used to good effect – the overriding consideration is that whatever material you use, it should not rot or corrode too quickly. Most materials deteriorate over time and may need replacing, but regular maintenance can delay this for a very long time. Maintenance is also important from a safety point of view.

? If I create a bog garden how will I be able to get to the plants to look after them?

By their nature bog gardens are not the easiest of gardens to walk in. If the area is not too wide you may be able to reach the plants from the sides, but a wide bed, especially if it backs onto your pond, will be difficult to work on. It is possible to create a network of paths through a large area, and bark chippings make a good surface, both aesthetically and practically. In a small bog garden stepping stones are a better choice. They are not conspicuous and perform their function well without taking up too much valuable space. The cheapest method is to have two or three square pieces of board that you use as temporary stepping stones and move as you progress across the bog. This is no good for simply walking across the bed, but it is a good solution for more static tasks like weeding.

? How can I make a stepping stone path through my bog garden?

The easiest stepping stones are simply paving slabs laid at a walking pace apart. These can be whole slabs or large pieces of paving stone (*illustrated above*). You could lay one main path of these, plus a few odd ones scattered to allow further access among the plants.

Smaller slabs are more likely to sink if the soil is really soft, but they are less obtrusive than large ones. An alternative is to use sawn sections of tree trunk, which look natural and fit in with the overall appearance of a bog garden. Log sections are, however, likely to become slippery. Make them safer by covering the surface with some fine mesh wire netting or chicken wire. Staple this to the logs and it will provide a very good slip-proof surface.

Handrails

Large bridges can have built-in handrails without looking out of place, and if the bridge is large there is usually plenty of water or a large drop beneath it and the rails are essential. Handrails on smaller bridges present more of a style problem. When children and people who have walking difficulties are in the garden handrails will be important for safety. If a bridge is only two or three paces across and is relatively wide there is less need for safety rails (especially if you have not got them around the pond itself). However, safety must always be your first priority, and they should be installed if there is any doubt, irrespective of appearance.

Lighting

There is no need to light a pond at all, and many gardeners prefer their pool to be natural, which means that it is dark at night. Some people like to be able to enjoy their pool's presence at all times of the day, however, and they also appreciate the completely different appearance that an night-illuminated pond has to its day-time counterpart. There are several ways of lighting a pond. It can be floodlit, so that everything is visible, or it can be spotlit so that individual features are picked out while the rest remains hidden in mysterious shadows. Floating night-lights will create a romantic atmosphere, which would be suitable if you are having a dinner party on a nearby patio. Floating solar-powered lights are also available, and they can give around 6–8 hours of light.

? Do I need to buy special lamps to use in and around the pond?

Yes; it is absolutely essential that you do not try to use household lamps in the garden and anywhere near water. Fortunately, there is an increasingly wide range of lamps available for all manner of garden and pond use, from spotlights and downlights for individual features, to underwater lighting. You can also obtain fountains with integral spotlights, encased in waterproof casing, and also units that enable you to change the colour of the beam. These are readily available from aquatic centres and come with full instructions.

? What is the best way to light a pond?

There are two ways of lighting a pond: from above and from below. When lighting from above, you can set the lights high up – in trees, for example – so that the entire area is illuminated, or you can use spotlights to pick out individual features, such as specimen plants or ornaments. Or you can set them low so the light is thrown upwards, though shrubs, trees and other plants, so that dramatic shadows are cast. A problem with low-level lighting is that it can shine into the eyes, so do not position lamps where they might temporarily dazzle someone so that they stumble into unseen water.

Underwater lighting can be used to illuminate the water from the edge of the pond so that whole area is lit, or the lamps

Garden lighting

After the tinkling noise of wind chimes there can be few things more irritating for your neighbours than for their gardens to be lit by your indiscriminately and thoughtlessly positioned lights. When you light your garden, make sure that the light is directed within your own boundaries and show some consideration for your neighbours.

can be concentrated under features, such as a waterfall (illustrated above left) or a bridge. When it is lit from above (illustrated above) the surface of the water can seem dark and impenetrable. When it is lit from below you can see into the water and watch the fish and other creatures moving around.

? **It is difficult to look at the pond at night because the lights are dazzling. How can I put this right?**

Lights that are positioned so that they point upwards to illuminate trees or other features are likely to be the culprits. Try to position any lights that are high up so that they point downwards. If you want lights that point upwards – to the underside of a bridge, for example – use a spotlight rather than a floodlight so that there is less light spill. If you do use a floodlight, place it so that it is masked and as little stray light as possible escapes. One of the main problems with garden lighting is that inappropriately powerful lamps are used. Subtle lighting is

Cables for lights

As with the electricity supply for the pump in your pond, the cable for lighting in and around the pool must be safe. Armoured cable, laid in a trench at least 60cm (2ft) deep within a plastic conduit, covered with a row of something like roof tiles and identified by a strip of yellow and black tape, should be used in conjunction with waterproof adapters, switches and junction boxes. Each light should be used with a circuit breaker. A transformer that steps down the mains current to 12 volts is safer, but do not lay the cable where it could be damaged during regular garden maintenance or could be tripped over.

frequently much more attractive and far less dazzling. Experiment with the positions of your lights before you wire them into their final positions.

4 Plants for a Water Garden

Designing for water plants

continuing down to the water's edge and into the muddy margins as well as into and on to the water itself. This type of pond allows for the greatest choice of plants. A wildlife pond is often similar in scope to an informal pond, but it may well contain many more native plants, selected not so much for their beauty as for their value in providing a suitable environment for wildlife.

Whatever your preference, try not to swamp the pond completely. Leave some open water, both because it makes a good contrast (rather as a lawn is somewhere for the eye to rest among the busyness of the flowerbeds) and because it provides areas for fish to swim freely.

> **? I like water plants for their own sake. What type of pond should I build?**

You can grow a wide range of plants in any sort of pond. However, the type of plants you have and the way you use them will vary according to the style of pond. In a formal pond, for example, it is usual to include only a limited number of species and to use these tellingly. They may be tall iris-like plants, positioned in the corners of a rectangular pond, or a floating raft of one or two waterlilies in the centre of a round pond. An informal pond, on the other hand, could be a riot of plants, with the planted banks

> **? I love water plants but do not want a pond. Can I grow them in other parts of the garden?**

Many water plants can be grown in ordinary beds and borders as long as the soil is not allowed to dry out, which can be achieved by adding plenty of humus to the soil. You will not, of course, be able to grow plants such as waterlilies without water, but many of the plants that can be grown in shallow water will also grow in reliably moist soil. Some will grow in ordinary beds, but others will do better if they are grown in a bog garden (see pages 28–9 and 44–5). Some plants, such as hostas and ferns, can be grown near to a water feature, such as a waterspout or pebble fountain, which has no open surface of water but where the air is moist and where drops of water will occasionally splash on to their leaves.

Water and waterside plants for beds and borders

The following will grow in good quality soil that does not dry out:

- *Astilbe* × *arendsii* cvs.
- *Caltha* spp. (marsh marigold, kingcup)
- *Dryopteris filix-mas* (male fern)
- *Hosta* cvs.
- *Houttuynia cordata*
- *Mimulus* spp. (musk, monkey flower)
- *Primula bulleyana* (candelabra primula)
- *Rheum palmatum* (Chinese rhubarb)
- *Rodgersia aesculifolia*
- *Trollius* × *cultorum* cvs. (globeflower)

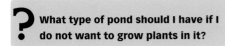

What type of pond should I have if I do not want to grow plants in it?

All ponds look naked without plants, but a formal pond, which is created for its outline rather than for its contents, will be most appropriate without any plants. If the pond looks too stark it can be enlivened with a fountain rather than with foliage and flowers. Semi-formal and informal ponds, on the other hand, depend on plants to break their edges and to give them life. Remember that if you want to keep fish you will have to install oxygenating equipment if you do not have any plants in the water.

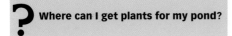

Where can I get plants for my pond?

The cheapest way to obtain plants is from friends and neighbours. However, this is not always the best way, no matter how well intentioned the offer, because the plants may come with hidden problems. Frequently, of course, people are only too glad to give away

bits of invasive plants, such as *Lemna* spp. (duckweed), so find out what you are being offered. Another drawback may be that the gift is harbouring algae, ready to colonize your own pond as soon as you put the plant in the water. If you want to accept the plant, check it thoroughly and wash off all the soil from around the roots so that you can get rid of any stray plants, unwelcome pests and unwanted seeds.

Although it is more expensive, a better way of obtaining plants for your pond is to buy them from a reputable specialist dealer, who will have an interest in maintaining a reputation for selling only healthy, good quality plants. A specialist aquatic dealer will also usually be able to advise you about the suitability of different plants for your pond size and on the hardiness and planting instructions of different species. Non-specialist nurseries and plant sales should be approached with caution.

Types of plant

? **What is the difference between the various types of water plant?**

Water plants are categorized according to the habitat in which they live. First are the submerged plants which are below water. They are also known as oxygenators because they supply the water with oxygen. Next are the deep-water plants (including waterlilies), which have long roots that go down to the bottom of the pond while the leaves and flowers are above water. These are followed by the floating plants, which have short roots. They get their nutrients from the topmost layer of water rather than from the mud in the bottom of the pond. Moving towards the sides of the pond, we find the marginals, which grow in the mud at varying depths of water around the pond's edge; some will also grow in moist soil and can be used in bog gardens. The next category are the waterside plants, which grow in moist soil near a pond but not actually in the water.

? **Do some plants need deeper water than others?**

Before you plant, always check the recommended planting depth, because some plants have adapted themselves for deeper water than others. Some are more adaptable than others and will grow in a wide range of depths. Usually, the planting depth given is the depth of water above a plant's crown and not the actual depth of a pond, and for this reason planting ledges and, if possible, sloping bottoms are used to provide a variety of planting depths so that you can grow a wide range of plants.

Waterlilies are well known for needing to be grown in a particular depth of water, and it is generally recommended that a waterlily container should be stood on several bricks, which can be removed, one by one, so that the mature waterlily is in the appropriate depth of water.

Types of water plant
The following are the five main types of water plant. A well-planted pond will include some plants from each group.
• Submerged plants or oxygenators
• Deep-water plants (including waterlilies)
• Floating plants
• Marginal plants
• Waterside plants

? **Are there any plants I should avoid?**

There are some plants in every category that can become rampant, suppressing everything else in the water and soon filling the pond completely. If possible, avoid them altogether, but if you have plenty of time to spend on your pond, they can be grown as long as they

are controlled by being regularly and ruthlessly thinned out. Some plants that are extremely vigorous in and around a pond can be more easily controlled in the drier ground of a garden, but some, such as *Azolla filiculoides* (fairy moss, water fern), are not easy to control in the natural environment, so do not simply dump these plants in the wild where they might grow unchecked, killing native plants.

Many species from all around the world are available from aquatic centres, but they should be bought with caution. If they are left to their own devices, plants such as *Hydrocotyle ranunculoides* (floating marsh pennywort), *Elodea canadensis* (Canadian pondweed) and *Myriophyllum aquaticum* (parrot's feather, diamond milfoil) are capable of completely dominating a pond, and they are extraordinarily difficult to eradicate once they have become established. Even some plants that are local are too invasive for domestic ponds – *Typha latifolia* (bulrush), for example, is far too vigorous for most garden ponds and its questing roots are capable of damaging flexible liners.

Plants to avoid in small ponds

The following should be bought only after careful consideration, or completely avoided, if you have a small pond:

- *Azolla filiculoides* (syn. *A. caroliniana*; fairy moss, water fern)
- *Elodea canadensis* (Canadian pondweed), illustrated left
- *Glyceria maxima* var. *variegata* (syn. *G. aquatica* var. *variegata*; variegated water grass)
- *Lemna* spp. (duckweed)
- *Myriophyllum aquaticum* (syn. *M. brasiliense*) *M. proserpinacoides*; parrot's feather, diamond milfoil)
- *Typha latifolia* (bulrush)

these in your pond even if they do not add to its visual attraction.

Submerged plants

? **What is a submerged plant?**

A submerged plant is one that will grow below the surface of the water. It may seem pointless to grow plants that you can hardly see and that do not appear to have any flowers, but these plants are essential to the well-being of your pond. They produce oxygen, which is held in the water, and this not only keeps the water 'sweet' but also provides a life source for a wide range of creatures, including fish. Submerged plants are, therefore, also known as oxygenating plants or oxygenators. The submerged plants compete with algae for nutrients, and they also provide valuable shelter for spawning fish. If you want a well-balanced pond it is important that you grow at least some of

Unfortunately, some of the plants used as oxygenators are rather rampant and will take over the whole pond if they are not kept under control. One of the worst offenders is *Elodea canadensis* (Canadian pondweed), (*illustrated above*), but it is one of the most reliable oxygenators and is also one of the most widely sold in aquatic centres. If you are prepared to pull out quantities of the weed once or twice every summer, either by hand or by dragging it out with a rake (*illustrated above left*), leaving behind enough to continue oxygenating, you might find that it works for you. Remember to check through the weed you have pulled out to ensure that you have not pulled out any fish or other creatures.

Submerged plants

The following submerged plants (oxygenators) should be available from large aquatic suppliers.

- *Callitriche* (starwort)
- *Ceratophyllum demersum* (hornwort), illustrated above right
- *Eleocharis acicularis* (hair grass)
- *Elodea canadensis* (Canadian pondweed), illustrated opposite right
- *Fontinalis antipyretica* (willow moss, water moss)
- *Hottonia palustris* (water violet), illustrated above left
- *Myriophyllum aquaticum* (parrot's feather, diamond milfoil)
- *Potamogeton crispus* (curled pondweed)

? How do I plant them?

Most submerged plants do not need to be planted in a pot in the conventional way. You buy them in bunches of stems rather than as a 'plant'. If there isn't already a piece of lead tied around them, fasten a small weight (even a stone will do) to the stems and simply drop them into the water.

? How many oxygenators do I need?

A pond which has been created in a half-barrel will need no more than one or two plants, but if you have a larger pond, introduce several species so that the planting density is at a rate of one bunch for every 30 × 30cm (1 × 1ft) or so of surface water, excluding marginal shelves.

Floating plants

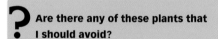
A floating plant is, as the name suggests, one that floats on the surface of the water, often forming large rafts. The plants have short roots, which hang down in the water but do not reach as far as the bottom of the pond. They obtain sufficient nutrients from the water and have no need to obtain them from the mud at the bottom. Apart from one or two species, floating plants are not particularly showy, but they play an important role in a well-balanced pond, covering areas of the surface to give fish and other creatures shade and protection from sun and predators, while leaving plenty of free unimpeded water below them.

Are there any of these plants that I should avoid?

In the right conditions, all of the plants listed here will spread indefinitely, although you need do no more than simply net them off when they become a nuisance. One of the worst offenders is *Azolla filiculoides* (fairy moss, water fern), a low, carpeting plant with pretty, lacy, red-tinted foliage. It looks especially attractive in smaller ponds, but it does spread like wildfire. In the garden it can be kept to reasonable dimensions by removing some of it from time to time, and fortunately it is not reliably hardy, so it is naturally controlled in very cold winters. In the wild it can cause havoc by choking streams and natural ponds, so never discard any plants in the wild. Most forms of *Lemna* (duckweed) can be a nuisance, too, covering the pond with a uniform, almost impenetrable carpet of

green (*illustrated left*). Apart from *L. trisulca* (ivy-leaved duckweed), which can be controlled by netting off, do not introduce duckweed into your pond.

Unfortunately, duckweed is likely to appear, anyway, carried in on the feet of a visiting bird or on a new plant, so you may not be able to escape it.

? How do I plant them?

It could not be easier: gently launch them on to the surface of the water. Some of these plants are tender or only half-hardy, and if your pond is in a cold, exposed place it would be a good idea to take a few pieces of plant out and keep them a frost-free place over winter, such as a cool greenhouse. This will make sure that you have some new plants for the following year in case a severe frost kills off all the plants in the pond.

? How many floating plants should I have?

Your aim should be to have a total of about one-third of the surface of the water covered with foliage, but some of this cover may be provided by deep-water aquatics, including waterlilies (see pages 84–5 and 86–7). Because most of the floating plants listed here will spread rapidly, they should be used to provide cover early in the season, before the deep-water plants and waterlilies come into full leaf.

Floating plants

The following floating plants are decorative and useful. Of those listed here, only *Marsilea quadrifolia* and *Stratiotes aloides* are hardy.

- *Azolla filiculoides* (syn. *A. caroliniana*; fairy moss, water fern)
- *Eichhornia crassipes* (water hyacinth), illustrated left
- *Hydrocharis morsus-ranae* (frogbit)
- *Lemna trisulca* (ivy-leaved duckweed)
- *Marsilea quadrifolia* (water clover), illustrated top
- *Pistia stratiotes* (water lettuce, shell flower)
- *Stratiotes aloides* (water soldier)
- *Utricularia vulgaris* (greater bladderwort)

Deep-water plants

? What are deep-water plants?

The plants in this group are similar to the floating plants described on pages 82–3, and many of them have similar almost round leaves. However, they differ in having roots that extend down into the mud at the bottom of the pond. One of the best-known examples of a deep-water plant is the waterlily, of which there are hundreds of varieties from which to choose, but there are other attractive plants that serve the same purpose.

? Why should I grow deep-water plants?

In addition to providing useful cover on the water's surface, which helps to shade out algae, deep-water plants tend to be more colourful than either floating or submerged plants because they often have flowers, which are sometimes, as in the case of the waterlily, quite large.

Unlike waterlilies, the deep-water aquatics listed here can be grown in ponds with moving water and they are more tolerant of shade or partial shade.

? How do I plant them?

Deep-water plants need to be grown in a minimum of 30cm (1ft) of water and have their roots in soil of some kind. The normal way is to plant them in lattice baskets and then place them in the water (see pages 94–5); they can also be grown in the soil of ponds that have a good covering of earth.

Deep-water aquatics

The following plants will spread their leaves on the surface of the water, providing valuable shade. These plants are hardy and are a useful alternative to waterlilies if your garden does not receive sufficient sun for waterlilies to bloom. These plants will also tolerate moving water.

- *Aponogeton distachyos* (water hawthorn), illustrated left
- *Nuphar avena* (American spatterdock)
- *Nuphar japonica* (Japanese pondlily)
- *Nymphoides peltata* (water fringe) illustrated right
- *Orontium aquaticum* (golden club)
- *Persicaria amphibia* (willow grass, amphibious bistort)
- *Ranunculus aquatilis* (water crowfoot), illustrated below

Water pH

Just as the pH level of your garden soil can be measured, so can the degree of acidity and alkalinity of the water in your garden pool. Easy-to-use kits are available from aquatic suppliers. Among the causes of too high alkalinity (above pH 7) is lime seeping out of concrete that has not been properly sealed. If the pH levels gets too high, water plants are unable to absorb nutrients, notably iron, from the water and fish become vulnerable to various gill disorders. Too much acidity in the water makes it difficult for plants to absorb phosphates, making their leaves turn brown or yellow, and fish become vulnerable to other diseases. It is difficult to redress a severe imbalance in the pH level: the best solution is to empty the pond and repot the plants.

Waterlilies

? I would like to grow waterlilies. Do I need a deep pond?

Most waterlilies do best in fairly deep water, but there are a few miniature cultivars, and these can be grown in a small container, such as a sink or half-barrel. On the other hand, there are hundreds of cultivars that will grow in deeper water, and when you are selecting a waterlily it is important to check whether it is suitable for the depth of water in your pond, otherwise they will not grow.

? Is it true that waterlilies should not be planted under a fountain?

Waterlilies dislike water turbulence of any kind, and it is true that they should not be planted immediately beneath a fountain or waterfall, where the leaves will be continually splashed by droplets. You should also try to protect waterlilies from water turbulence caused by strong winds, perhaps by planting stands of rushes or sedges on the side of the pond from which the wind tends to blow most strongly.

? My pond seems to be filling up with waterlilies very quickly. Is there a similar plant I could use?

There are, literally, hundreds of different waterlilies. Some of these, as you have discovered, can be very rampant, but there are many that are much more restrained in their habit of growth, and if you want to continue with waterlilies it would be worth visiting a specialist aquatic centre to see what cultivars are available. The hardy waterlilies listed below have a spread of about 1.2m (4ft), so they should be suitable for most garden ponds. The planting depth indicated is for mature plants. Of course, it is possible to keep the existing lilies and cut them back each year. There are other floating and deep-water plants that you could use (see pages 82–3), but most of these will eventually expand to fill the available space.

- *Nymphaea* 'Firecrest': pink; 30–45cm (12–18in)
- *Nymphaea* 'Gonnère': white; 30–45cm (12–18in)
- *Nymphaea* 'James Brydon': rose-red; 30–45cm (12–18in)
- *Nymphaea* 'Marliacea Albida': white; 30–45cm (12–18in)
- *Nymphaea* 'Odorata Sulphurea Grandiflora': yellow; 30–45cm (12–18in)
- *Nymphaea* 'Pink Sensation': pink; 30–45cm (12–18in)
- *Nymphaea* 'Radiant Red': red; 30–45cm (12–18in)
- *Nymphaea* 'Vésuve': red; 30-45cm (12–18in)

- *Nymphaea* 'Virginalis': white; 37–45cm (15–18in)
- *Nymphaea* 'William Falconer': red; 45–75cm (18–30cm)

 Are special techniques needed to propagate waterlilies?

The easiest way to increase waterlilies is to lift them, divide the plant into individual crowns and replant it. This is not always possible and another way, and one that will produce many more plants, is to increase them from 'eyes' just as growth begins in early summer. These eyes are found on the rootstock and are usually in the form of small buds or growing tips. Use a sharp knife to remove as many of these as you require and then replant the plant. Plant the growing tips in individual pots of aquatic compost and stand them in a tray of water so that the compost is just covered with water. Pot on and plant them out, lowering them in the water as they grow.

Miniature waterlilies

The following hardy waterlilies can be grown in comparatively small containers. The planting depth indicated is the depth of water above the crown of the plant, not the overall depth of the pond:

- *Nymphaea* 'Aurora': cream-yellow flowers turning to orange-red; 30–45cm (12–18in)
- *Nymphaea* 'Ellisiana': fragrant, bright red flowers; 30–45cm (12–18in)
- *Nymphaea* 'Froebelii': dark red flowers; 30cm (1ft)
- *Nymphaea* 'Laydekeri Fulgens':

fragrant, crimson flowers; 30–45cm (12–18in)
- *Nymphaea* 'Paul Hariot': yellow to red; 15–30cm (6–12in)
- *Nymphaea* 'Pink Opal': pink; 15–23cm (6–9in)
- *Nymphaea* 'Pygmaea Helvola' (syn. *N. helvola*): clear yellow flowers; 15–23cm (6–9in)
- *Nymphaea* 'Pygmaea Rubra': deep pink; 15–23cm (6–9in)
- *Nymphaea* 'Ray Davies': pink; 30–45cm (12–18in)
- *Nymphaea tetragona* (syn. *N.* 'Pygmaea Alba'): white; 15–30cm (6–12in)

grow varies from squelchy mud up to about 30cm (1ft) or more. Some are tall plants, while other crawl across the surface of the mud or water. There is usually a good contrast of foliage shapes, from the tall, narrow leaves of irises and rushes to the wider leaves of *Lysichiton americanus* (yellow skunk cabbage).

? Are any marginal plants unsuitable for a small pond?

Some marginal plants, especially some of the native species, such as *Typha latifolia* (bulrush), can be very invasive and should not be grown in anything but the largest of ponds. A few of the grasses and sedges can also be rather invasive, but, as with all invasive garden plants, if you are prepared to keep them under control they can more than earn their place. Most other water plants will make large drifts or clumps, but are generally not invasive and are more easily controlled.

Marginals and waterside plants

? What are marginal plants?

Marginal plants are those that grow in the mud or shallow water around the edges of the pond. In a shallow pond they may even grown into the centre of the pond. All marginals will grow in standing or running water; some bog plants can be grown as marginals, but not all bog plants will grow in water. Marginal plants help to define and decorate the edges of the pond. They are important in all types of pond, but they work especially well in informal ponds, where drifts of plants around the margins add greatly to the effect.

The depth of water in which marginals will

? How should I plant them?

Marginal plants

The following plants are suitable for a small to medium pond. Although they are hardy, take care that spring frosts do not catch early flowers.

- *Caltha palustris* (marsh marigold, kingcup), illustrated opposite top
- *Cotula coronopifolia* (bachelor's buttons, golden buttons)
- *Iris laevigata* 'Variegata', stripy leaves illustrated below
- *Iris pseudacorus* (yellow flag, flag iris)
- *Lysichiton americanus* (yellow skunk cabbage)
- *Myosotis scorpioides* (syn. *M. palustris*; water forget-me-not)
- *Peltandra virginica* (syn. *P. undulata*; green arrow arum)
- *Pontederia cordata* (pickerel weed), illustrated left
- *Veronica beccabunga* (brooklime)

There are several ways of planting marginals, and the method varies according to the particular type of pond you have. If your pond has a liner, lattice pots can be used, and the pots can then be arranged on one of the marginal ledges, depending on the water depth required. If you pond has a layer of soil across the bottom the marginals can be planted directly into it: you can lean over carefully or put on some wellington boots and wade out to scoop a hole. If you know when you are designing your pond that you will want to grow a good range of marginal plants and you are planning to use a flexible liner, you could construct a pond with a special shallow ledge around part or all of the edge. The ledge could be filled with soil so that it is partly or totally below the water level, and this will be the perfect growing habitat for many marginal plants.

Tender aquatics

? Are all water plants hardy?

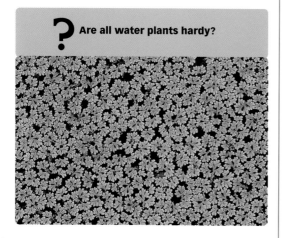

No; many attractive water plants, including some lovely waterlilies, sold at water centres are more suitable for growing in indoor ponds – those in conservatories, for example. Few of us have an indoor pool, however, and it is worth taking cuttings, divisions or whole plants and overwintering them in a frost-free place and putting them outside again when all fear of frost has passed. Some half-hardy

plants, such as *Azolla filiculoides* (fairy moss, water fern (*illustrated left*), and *Myriophyllum aquaticum* (parrot's feather, diamond milfoil), will spread indefinitely in the right conditions, and a cold winter will limit them to just a few plants and help to keep them under control. In is often possible to overwinter tender plants in many town gardens with enclosed courtyards, but it is always a wise precaution to take cuttings as an insurance.

? Which waterlilies are tender?

There are several lovely tender waterlilies, some blooming during the day, others blooming at night. Many are very fragrant. The following day-blooming waterlilies have blue flowers unless otherwise indicated: *Nymphaea* 'Aviator Pring' (yellow flowers); *N.* 'Blue Beauty' (fragrant); *N. caerulea* (blue lotus) (*illustrated right*); *N. capensis* (Cape blue waterlily); *N. capensis* 'Rosea' (pink flowers); *N.* × *daubenyana*; *N.* 'General Pershing' (bluish-pink flowers); *N. gigantea* (Australian

Tender water plants

The following water plants are tender and will not survive outdoors all year round if the winter temperature falls below –1–4°C (30–40°F) for more than a couple of days.

- *Anubias afzelii*
- *Cabomba caroliniana* (Carolina water shield)
- *Colocasia esculenta* (taro)
- *Cyperus haspan*
- *Egeria densa*
- *Eichhornia crassipes* (water hyacinth)
- *Myriophyllum aquaticum* (syn. *M. brasiliense*, *M. proserpinacoides*; parrot's feather, diamond milfoil)
- *Nelumbo* spp. (sacred lotus), illustrated right
- *Pistia stratiotes* (water lettuce, shell flower)
- *Trapa natans* (water caltrops or chestnut), illustrated left

waterlily); *N.* 'Independence' (rose-pink flowers); *N. lotus* (Egyptian waterlily; pink-tinged white flowers, sometimes night blooming); *N. mexicana* (yellow waterlily; yellow flowers); and *N.* 'St Louis' (fragrant, yellow flowers). The following bloom at night: *N. 'Emily Grant Hutching' (dark pink flowers); N. 'Red Flare' (dark red flowers);* N. 'Sir Galahad' (white flowers); and *N.* 'Wood's White Knight' (white flowers).

Gardeners who do not have the facilities to overwinter tender waterlilies but who grow them for the fragrance or colour often treat them as annuals.

Planting around the pond

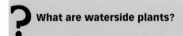 **What are waterside plants?**

Waterside plants are those plants that can be grown beside water but not in it. If the nearby border is a bog garden then the associated plants will be bog plants (see pages 28–9), but in many cases the plants will be ordinary border plants growing in ordinary border soil. Some of these plants are associated with moist soils – *Aruncus dioicus* (syn. *A. sylvestris*; goatsbeard) and hostas, for example – and they are ideal for this kind of position. Some are ordinary border plants, such as *Alchemilla mollis* (lady's mantle), which look wonderful when they are grown on a dry bank so that they tumble down over the water's edge.

Several trees and shrubs can also be used in this setting, the classic example being *Salix babylonica* (weeping willow), but do take care if you plant this, because it will grow into a very large tree and needs a lot of space to be seen at its best. There are many others to choose from.

Do I plant them in the conventional way?

Yes; the borders are conventional ones that just happen to be next to water, so they should be planted in the normal way. Prepare the soil thoroughly, digging in plenty of well-rotted organic material.

Dig a hole slightly bigger than the rootball of the plant. Place the plant in the centre of the hole and spread out the roots. It should be planted at the same depth as the plant was in its pot or in its previous planting. Fill in gently around the roots with soil and then firm down well and water thoroughly.

? There are too many yellow plants round my pond. Which blue flowers would be suitable?

There are several blue-flowered plants and these go very well with water, although they are more muted than the yellows. The following can be grown as marginals:

- *Iris laevigata*
- *Iris versicolor*
- *Myosotis scorpioides* (syn. *M. palustris*; water forget-me-not)
- *Pontederia cordata* (pickerel weed)
- *Veronica beccabunga* (brooklime)

These blue-flowered plants can be grown in reliably moist soil but will not grow if they are in permanently wet conditions:

- *Cardamine pratense* (lady's smock, cuckoo flower)
- *Iris ensata* (syn. *I. kaempferi*)
- *Iris sibirica*
- *Lobelia gerardii* 'Vedrariensis'
- *Primula* spp.

? Can I apply chemical fertilizers and insecticides to the plants around my pond?

It is better not to apply chemicals of any kind in the vicinity of your pond; if there are fish the slightest contamination of the water will affect them. One of the causes of algal growth is raised nitrogen levels caused by run-off from garden fertilizers. No matter how carefully you plan the borders, it is almost inevitable that in periods of heavy rain some fertilizer will leach into the pond water. It is better to rely on garden compost and manure.

Plants for the waterside

The following plants are suitable for growing in borders and beds next to your pond. These are not aquatic plants and they will not grow if their roots are in permanently wet soil:

- *Alchemilla mollis* (lady's mantle)
- *Blechnum spicant* (hard fern)
- *Cornus alba* (red dogwood), illustrated right
- *Cornus stolonifera* (red osier dogwood)
- *Geum rivale* (avens)
- *Hosta* cvs.
- *Leucojum aestivum* (summer snowflake)
- *Primula* spp., illustrated above right
- *Rheum palmatum* (Chinese rhubarb)
- *Rodgersia aesculifolia*

Planting water plants

? How do I plant when there is no soil in the pond?

Although it is possible to place a layer of soil over a liner and plant into this, most gardeners prefer to plant in containers. This has several advantages: it is easier to plant away from the sides of the pond; it is easier to remove the plant and split it up without having to dig it from the bottom of the pool, which might damage the liner; and the containers help to restrict the invasive nature of some water plants, and keep them in discreet clumps.

Most ponds are constructed in such a way that there are planting ledges and sloping sides, so that there is a variety of planting depths and positions on which containers can be positioned.

? What are the best types of containers for planting in ponds?

The containers used for water plants are like plastic flower pots except that the sides are made of lattice or mesh so that water can pass in and out of the roots of the plant without going stale. They are usually called aquatic baskets, and the open sides also allow the roots to spread out of the confines of the container into the water. Unfortunately, the compost can also pass out through the basket, and this problem overcome by lining the it with a square of hessian or woven polypropylene, which is available from water centres.

Recently very fine, louvre-type mesh baskets have appeared on the market. These require no lining and are available in a good range of sizes.

? How is the aquatic basket filled?

Choose a container that is big enough to contain the rootball of the plant. If it has open mesh sides, line it with a piece of hessian or woven polypropylene. Hold the plant in the centre of the pot and fill in around the roots with compost, gently firming down as you go so that the roots are completely surrounded with soil and there are no air pockets. The level of the soil should be about 1cm (½in) below the rim of the pot. Cover the compost with a thick layer of gravel, which will help hold both the compost and the plant in place,

Compost for water plants

Do not use soil-less composts for water plants, because the light, fibrous material will quickly float to the surface of the pond, leaving the plants' roots bare. Buy special aquatic compost, which is soil-based and specially formulated for use under water.

Sinking a planting basket in deep water

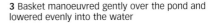

3 Basket manoeuvred gently over the pond and lowered evenly into the water

1 Strings threaded through sides of planting basket and laid across surface of soil

2 Basket lifted carefully by one person on each side

preventing them from floating away.

The gravel will also help to deter fish from nosing about in the surface of the soil. Water thoroughly to remove the air and place the container in the pond.

? **How do I get plants into the middle of the pond?**

Plants that will stand around the edge of the pond can be simply lowered into place as long as you can reach without falling in, but it is more difficult to position plants in the centre of a large pond.

If you do not want to put on your wellington boots and wade in, one of the best ways – which needs two people – is to run two long pieces of stout string through the mesh at the top of the container. If each person holds one end of both pieces of string, it is possible to support the basket on the strings. One person walks to the other side of the pond so that the pot is suspended over the water in the middle of the pond. Adjust

your position so that the pot is in the right place and then lower it slowly and carefully into the water, taking care that it does not tip up. Once the basket has sunk into place, one person releases their ends, and the other gently pulls the string out of the container.

? **When I put a basket with a plant in it in the water, all the compost and then the plant floated to the surface. What did I do wrong?**

You used the wrong compost. Ordinary soil-less compost, which is the mainstay of most container gardening, is composed mainly of fibrous material, which will float when it is immersed in water. In future, use either a specially formulated aquatic compost from your local water gardening centre or use a soil-based potting compost. As a further insurance, when you have potted up the plant, make sure that you cover the surface with a good layer of gravel to hold the compost and the plant safely in place in the basket.

Propagation

? Is it easy to propagate water plants?

Propagating water plants is no more difficult than propagating any other type of garden plant. Bog plants, marginals and waterside plants are all propagated in the conventional ways, by seed, division or cuttings. True aquatic plants present more of a problem: because they grow in water they have to be propagated in water, which involves keeping them in trays of water.

? Is seed sown in the same way as conventional seed?

More or less. Fill a pot with aquatic compost and spread the seeds evenly across the surface. Cover these with a 5mm (¼in) layer of fine grit. Water thoroughly. With most plants the pot is then placed in a shady position until the seed germinates, but if the seed comes from true bog plants, stand the pot in a container of water, so that the water level is part-way up the pot. If the seed came from water plants, such as waterlilies, stand the pot in water that comes over the top of the gravel and keep it topped up.

Plants to grow from seed

The following water plants can be propagated from seed:

- *Alisma plantago-aquatica* (water plantain)
- *Baldellia ranunculoides*
- *Calla palustris* (bog arum)
- *Cotula coronopifolia* (bachelor's buttons, golden buttons)
- *Cyperus longus*
- *Mimulus luteus* (monkey musk)
- *Myosotis scorpioides* (syn. *M. palustris*; water forget-me-not)
- *Nymphaea* spp. (not cultivars, which are mostly sterile)
- *Orontium aquaticum* (golden club)

Plants for division

The following plants are among those that can be easily divided:

- *Acorus calamus* (sweet flag, myrtle flag)
- *Aponogeton distachyos* (water hawthorn, Cape pondweed)
- *Caltha palustris* 'Flore Pleno', illustrated top right
- *Eriophorum angustifolium* (common cotton grass)
- *Glyceria maxima* var. *variegata* (syn. *G. aquatica* var. *variegata*; variegated water grass)
- *Houttuynia cordata*
- *Iris* spp., *Iris ensata* illustrated bottom right
- *Mentha aquatica* (water mint)
- *Peltandra sagittifolia* (syn. *P. alba*; white arrow arum)
- *Primula* spp., illustrated opposite

Plants from cuttings

The following aquatic plants can be propagated by cuttings:

- *Calla palustris* (bog arum)
- *Callitriche hermaphroditica* (syn. *C. autumnalis*; autumnal starwort)
- *Elodea canadensis* (Canadian pondweed)
- *Fontinalis antipyretica* (willow moss, water moss)
- *Hottonia palustris* (water violet)
- *Mentha aquatica* (water mint)
- *Menyanthes trifoliata* (bog bean, marsh trefoil)
- *Myriophyllum aquaticum* (syn. *M. brasiliense, M. proserpinacoides*; parrot's feather, diamond milfoil)
- *Potamogeton crispus* (curled pondweed)

? How can I divide water plants?

This is a relatively simple procedure. First, dig up the plant or remove it from the water. Wash off the soil from around the roots and use your fingers to work parts of the plant apart gently. Many plants fall apart easily into separate plants, but others need a bit more persuasion and may need to be cut into sections, each of which should have an active bud. Hold the division in a pot and fill this with aquatic compost, firming it down so that the compost comes up to the same level as before. Cover the compost with grit and water. Most plants should be kept under cover for a few weeks until they have re-established themselves and are ready either for placing in open frames or planting out. Water plants will need to be placed in trays of water to keep them wet.

? Is it possible to take cuttings of water plants?

Some water plants respond readily to being taken as cuttings. The simplest are the submerged plants: take a few stems, tie them together in a bundle with a strip of lead or a stone and drop them into the water. They sink to the bottom and will soon take root. Some plants, such as *Calla palustris* (bog arum), can be increased if you take cuttings from the creeping stems and place sections of them, each containing a bud, in a pot of wet compost and then place this in a tray of water. Conventional stem cuttings can be taken from a wide range of marginal and bog plants, such as *Mentha aquatica* (water mint).

? What are turions?

Turions are fleshy buds, which are produced in order to carry the plant through winter by storing food. These fall naturally from some plants and float off to create a new one. Sometimes, however, the gardener has to remove the turion from its parent and plant it in a pot of wet compost and keep it under water. Among the plants that can be increased from turions are *Butomus umbellatus* (flowering rush) and *Hottonia palustris* (water violet).

Pests and diseases

Many of the plants in my pond are wilting. What is wrong?

The most likely cause is that you have used the wrong plants. Not all plants will grow in water, and ordinary garden plants hate to be permanently wet, even if they like a moist soil. They must have free drainage around their roots. Planting them in the water or in the soaking soil of a bog garden will make them flag and eventually die.

The plants may be diseased. Inspect them thoroughly to see if there is any evidence of pests or disease. If there is, remove the plants from the pond. Do not use ordinary garden sprays on water plants because they may contain chemicals that are injurious to fish and other water creatures. It is worth remembering that diseases are not as common as one might think, and if several different types of plant are involved the chances are it is not this. Careless spraying of weeds, even some distance off, may have caused spray to drift on to plants and cause them to go pale without actually killing them. The safest thing to do is to remove the plants and replace them next season with new ones.

What has caused the brown spots on the leaves of my waterlily?

The probable cause is waterlily leaf spot (*illustrated below*), a fungal problem that can be disfiguring but is rarely fatal. The problem arises if you do not immediately notice the problem and the leaves are left to rot, which can happen quickly in warm weather. As soon as you notice the spots, remove the leaves and burn them.

What is waterlily crown rot?

This is probably the most serious disease that can occur in an ornamental pond. The fungus causes the stems and crown to turn black and rot. It is a virulent infection, which will spread quickly from waterlily to waterlily. Remove and burn affected plants.

The leaves of my lily are covered with tiny black flies. What should I do?

Waterlily aphids *(illustrated above)* are a nuisance, and if you allow large colonies to become established they can even kill plants by sucking the sap of the leaves and flowers. The best way to get rid of them is to direct a strong jet of water from a garden hose on to the leaves. The fish will then eat the aphids.

The aphids overwinter on plum and cherry trees, so if you have these trees in your garden, remember to apply a tar oil wash.

What has been eating the leaves of my waterlilies?

The most likely culprits are waterlily beetles, which are about twice as large as a ladybird and dark brown. It is the larvae that feed on the lily pads, causing the leaves to disintegrate, and three or four broods of larvae can be hatched in a year. Spray the leaves with a strong jet of water to remove the pests, so that the fish eat them, and remove the foliage. It is a good idea to tidy up the foliage of herbaceous perennials around the pool's edge in autumn so that there are fewer places for the adults to overwinter. There is also a parasitic bacterium, *Bacillus thuringiensis*, which is available through specialist suppliers; it is completely harmless to fish.

5 Introducing Wildlife

Attracting wildlife

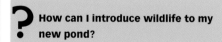
How long do I have to wait before I can stock the pond with plants and wildlife?

Unless you have filled your pond with rainwater, it is likely that you will have coupled a garden hose to the mains. This water usually contains chlorine and possibly other chemicals, and it should be left to stand for at least a week so that these can disperse before you attempt to plant up your pond and

add wildlife. It is also a good idea to wait until the plants have established themselves before any wildlife is added to the pond.

How can I introduce wildlife to my new pond?

It is surprising how little needs to be done, because most wildlife will find it themselves as long as you have provided the sort of habitat they like. You may even find that as you fill the pond, pond skaters arrive before you have more than a few centimetres in the bottom, and dragonflies will appear as if from nowhere. Frogs will eventually find their way to the water, but introducing frogspawn will speed up the process and any frogs born of that spawn will return to the pond to spawn themselves once they have matured. Many small creatures are accidentally introduced into the pond on waterweed, especially if you got it from a friend's pond instead of from a garden centre. Fish are the one thing that are slow to arrive, but even these may eventually appear, perhaps carried as eggs on a visiting bird's foot. So, apart from possibly introducing frogspawn, the only thing to introduce if you want them is fish (see pages 102–3).

? Wildlife does not come to my pond. What have I done wrong?

There may be several reasons for this. The first is that the pond may be too new for them to have found it yet: they will not necessarily turn up on the first day. The second is that the pond may not have sufficient suitable plants. An empty pond is less likely to attract wildlife than one with plenty of vegetation. Sometimes, especially if your garden is in the centre of a city, the pond is too far away from existing colonies for the creatures to arrive by themselves, but it is surprising how far they do travel. There is also the possibility that they may be there but you have not seen them yet. Many are surprisingly elusive.

? I have found dead small mammals in the pond. Is there anything I can do to stop this happening?

The main problem that small animals face with a pond is getting into the water and not being able to get out. Many can swim, reluctantly, if their life depends on it, but the problem is often that they cannot climb out of a steep-sided pond, especially if the edge is overhung with paving slabs.

If you can provide one or more ramps the animals will be able to climb out. Even a log propped up between the edge of the pond and the water will enable them to escape from the water.

Fish

? **Can fish be housed in an ordinary garden pond?**

Fish can be kept in any pond as long as it does not become overcrowded and as long as the water has enough oxygen. You have only to think that goldfish are kept in bowls, and you will realize that even a small pond will offer a far better environment for them, and if you create a natural habitat with plenty of oxygenating plants and plenty of other plants to provide cover and shelter, you will create a balanced pond in which fish should thrive without further attention.

Overcrowding should not be a problem unless the pond is a small one and the fish breed at a vigorous rate. Aim to have no more than 5cm (2in) of fish for every 30 × 30cm (1 × 1ft) of water surface. The quality of the water can also be a problem, especially in a small pond. The water can kept oxygenated by using oxygenating plants (see pages 80–81), but if you have a pond with no plants but you want to keep ornamental fish, you will have to have a filtration system of some sort. Ask your local water plant or fish centre for advice on the most suitable system.

? **What types of fish can I have?**

There are two main types of fish. Ornamental ones include those with coloured scales, such as koi, and native ones would normally be found in local ponds. Local ones have a better chance of adapting and will need no attention, generally breeding quite happily once they have settled in. The more usual ornamental fish, such as goldfish, will probably also not cause any problems once they are used to their environment, but if you are interested in keeping koi (*illustrated above right*), you

should consider keeping them in special ponds, where the conditions can be carefully monitored. They can be housed in a garden pool but they will often graze on the plant life.

? **Which fish need the least attention?**

In a properly built pool most fish will need little attention. If the pond is big enough you will not even have to feed them. Native fish in particular can be simply left to get on with it, but even more exotic fish, such as goldfish, are happy without any attention as long as they are not overcrowded.

Breeding fish

Most fish will breed naturally in the pond without you having to do anything. If you keep koi you may need to have a special breeding pool, where they can safely multiply.

? Where do I get fish?

You may have a neighbour or friend who has plenty of fish in their pool and would be willing to let you have a few. The problem with this is that you may unwittingly be introducing diseased livestock into your pond. If you go to one of the reputable fish or water garden centres you will find a large range of fish and will be able to get advice on what would be best for your needs. Reputable retailers will normally have disease-free stock and healthy fish. When you are buying, it is preferable to get several small fish rather than a few large ones. Young fish settle in more quickly than older ones.

? Do I need to feed fish?

In a well-balanced pond containing plenty of different plants and creatures there should be no need to feed your fish, but for many pond owners this is part of the fun of keeping fish and, regularly fed, they will soon learn to come as they hear you approach. The main problem is what to feed them. There is a bewildering choice of foodstuff at water centres, and it is best to seek advice when you buy the fish.

Do not give too much food at any time because as it decays it will pollute the water. Something like stick food is good as it floats and can easily be removed if it is not eaten.

? How do I get the fish into the pond?

It is most likely that you will bring the fish home in a large polythene bag. Place or hang this in the pond for at least an hour so that the temperature of the water in the bag slowly drops to that of that of the pool to allow the fish to acclimatize rather than getting the sudden shock of cold water after the warmth of the water centre. Do not leave the sealed bag in sunlight or the temperature will rise rapidly and the oxygen run out. Once the temperature has stabilized, open the bag, push it below water and gently allow its water and the fish to mix with that of the pond. The fish are likely to disappear to the bottom of the pond until they get used to their new home, so do not assume that they have all been eaten.

Fish for an outdoor pond

The following fish can be kept in an ordinary outdoor pool. Most fish will cohabit happily with other species, but catfish can sometimes be aggressive, so try to keep them away from other species.

- Carp, including koi, higoi
- Catfish
- Dace
- Goldfish, including fantails, moors, comets and lionheads
- Orfe, silver and golden forms
- Roach, illustrated right
- Rudd, silver and golden forms
- Shubunkin, including comet-tailed types
- Tench

Insects and molluscs

? What insects are likely to visit my pond?

The most attractive insects that will visit a pond are dragonflies (*illustrated right*) and damselflies. There is no need to introduce them: they will just appear and soon breed in the pond, giving you years of pleasure.

Encourage them by making sure there is plenty of vegetation on and in the pond to provide them with landing places as well as places to lay eggs, hide as larvae from the fish and eventually to dry their wings once they emerge into their final, most beautiful stage.

Not all insects are as attractive as dragonflies. Mosquitoes (*illustrated top right*) may also breed in your pond, but the dragonfly larvae and fish will eat the nymphs and keep the populations under control.

? There are wasps and insects on my floating lily pads. What are they doing and are they dangerous?

Wasps, like other creatures, need water, both to live by and for mixing with the material from which they build their nests. They are simply using the lilies as landing pads from which they have easy access to water. They should cause you no harm as long as you leave them alone.

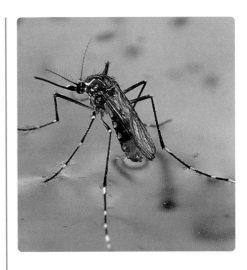

? **How should I introduce water snails?**

Whether snails in the pond are a good thing is a much debated point. Snails are sold in aquatic centres and introduced into ponds because they play a scavenging role, removing algae, decaying plant material, excess fish food and even dead fish and worms. Those known as ramshorn snails, *Planorbis corneus*, which have a flattened, wheel-like shell, will perform these useful tasks, as will the black Japanese snail, *Viviparis malleatus*.

Other snails can be a nuisance and will eat up plant leaves, just like their land-based cousins do, and these are best avoided. If you want water snails to add to the balance of your pond, seek them out from the more reputable garden centres to make certain that you get the right ones. If your pond becomes infested with unwelcome snails, leave a few lettuce or cabbage leaves floating on the water overnight. You will be able to remove the snails and what remains of the leaves in the morning.

Amphibians and reptiles

How can I introduce tadpoles to my pond?

Frogs and tadpoles are now in short supply, and gone are the days when you could go to the local pond with a jamjar and fill it up with frogspawn. If you have patience frogs will find their way to your pond and soon start breeding there. They have a tendency to come back to the same pond to breed, so once they start they will continue to come back, especially if they were born there. You can precipitate the situation if you know somebody with a pond that has plenty of frogspawn in it from which you can take a little and add it to your own pond. What you should not do is to raid natural ponds in your neighbourhood, because any spawn you see there should be left to develop in natural conditions to replenish the countryside.

There were nearly 40 frogs in my pond this spring. Should I try to thin them out?

Ponds swarming with frogs are quite a common sight in spring when all the frogs return to their favourite pond to breed. The water suddenly seems to be alive with them. There is no need to be alarmed or take any action. They will mate, produce frogspawn and then disappear again as suddenly as they arrived.

Can I have newts in my pond?

Whether you want them or not, newts are almost certain to turn up as soon as the pond is clothed with plants. It is sometimes difficult to know where they arrive from, and they are thought to cover some considerable distance. Sometimes ponds can seem overcrowded with newts, and if you know someone who

has too many you can transfer some, as long as your pond is mature and ready to receive them. But the best policy is to wait and watch: they will arrive on their own.

They will do no harm – indeed, they eat many garden pests – and are delightful creatures to watch as they surface for air and then dive down again.

? Do toads live in ponds?

Toads only enter water to breed. They tend not to be as noticeable as frogs, mainly because they are more active at night. They like to live in damp, cool positions under stones or other cover. If you provide a few

such places in the garden they are likely to appear, but you will have to keep a keen eye to spot them. They are welcome additions, eating huge numbers of slugs and caterpillars.

? I have seen grass snakes swimming in my pond. Are they safe?

If you regularly watch your pond, especially if it is designed for wildlife, you will see the occasional grass snake cross it (*illustrated above*). They will cause you no harm. Grass snakes will eat the occasional frog or fish, but they are unlikely to upset the balance of the pond, indeed they enhance it. If you are really frightened of snakes, get somebody who isn't to remove it for you – but don't kill it.

Mammals and birds

❓ How can I make a small pond for birds to bathe in?

Birds do not need much water – a small puddle will do – but to make access easy for them you can provide a permanent place for them to get to the water in the form of a ramp or you can make a separate bathing place. Traditionally birdbaths are shallow stone or cement dishes on a plinth, but an easy alternative is to sink a dustbin lid or some other shallow container in the lawn and keep this filled with water. Place some flat stones in it so that the birds have somewhere to stand. They appreciate it if it is out in the open rather than surrounded by plants so that they can see any approaching predators at what, for them, is a vulnerable time.

❓ Can I build nest boxes for waterbirds?

Most ducks find their own nest sites, often far away from water, which are usually on or near the ground and hidden in vegetation. Some ducks nest in holes in trees and are unlikely to use a box placed on or by the water, although you may be lucky if there are no appropriate

A bathing platform for birds

A simple bathing platform can be created from a piece of wood or log. It can just be thrown in the water but it is better if it can be anchored with a piece of rot-proof string attached to a stone, so that it does not blow to the edge of the pond.

sites around. The birds that are more likely to use such a box are domesticated fowl that live permanently around the pond and cannot fly off to a distant nest site. You need provide nothing more than a four-sided box with a sloping roof and a large entrance hole, positioned so that the opening faces away from the prevailing wind and rain (*illustrated above*). If it can be built out over the water or on an island, away from predators such as cats and foxes, so much the better.

? How can non-swimming birds bathe or drink from a pond?

Most garden birds bathe in water or fine dust, and those that choose water are often content with something as shallow as a puddle. Ponds are usually too deep for them, but if you can, provide something for the birds to stand on so that they are out of reach of most predators. You can create small floating platforms on the water; these must be low so that birds can reach the surface of the water. Alternatively, you can stand a stone on a piece of underlay in the shallows of the pond.

Ideally, it should have a flattish top and a gently sloping side so that birds reach the edge of the water, even if the water level drops. Some birds are small and light enough to land and bathe on lily pads.

? I have found a dead hedgehog in my pond. Can they swim and how can I help them get out?

Hedgehogs frequently fall into ponds, often when they are attempting to drink but sometimes simply because they want to get to the other side. They can swim and usually manage to get out. However, if the sides of your pond are steep and the bank is well above the water level or if the edge of the pond is overhung all round with paving, it is difficult and often impossible for them to climb out and, sadly, they eventually drown. You can help them by building a ramp from the bank down to the water level. A log or flat piece of wood will do, if you are unable to flatten the bank itself. Such a ramp will be of use to a wide range of animals that may fall in the water or want access to it to drink.

Predators and other problems

? Are fish prone to lots of pests and diseases?

As long as the water does not become fetid or frozen, fish generally remain healthy in an outdoor pool. There is always the risk that if you add new fish to a pond you will introduce a problem, but generally it is a sealed community, and if the fish are healthy to begin with and the pond is well balanced they are unlikely to suffer from any problems. The worst disease you are likely to encounter is white spot, which is sometimes introduced on newly bought fish and which is particularly prevalent in warm weather. There are

chemicals that can be added to the water, which must only be used according to the manufacturer's instructions. Other common problems include fungus (cotton wool disease), which affects fish that are damaged in some way: make sure there are no sharp, protruding edges in your pond.

? A heron keeps eating my fish. How can I prevent this?

Grey herons (*illustrated above*) are very determined birds, and they can be a nuisance once they have discovered a good source of food because they will keep on coming back. Make sure there is plenty of cover around the margins of the pool with clear water in the centre, where the water will be too deep for the heron to wade. There are a number of proprietary guards, which rely on the bird pressing against an inconspicuous cord to release a sprung device that sets off a small cap or other sound. Another solution is to erect a series of low-level wires around the edge of the pond so that the heron cannot wade into the pond from the bank, which is their preferred method of fishing. If all else fails, you might have to lay plastic netting over the entire surface (*illustrated below*).

? **How do I keep cats away from my pond?**

There is no need to take any steps to keep cats away from your pond. Cats can swim if they fall in, although they rarely choose to get into the water, so if you are worried about your cat's safety, make sure it can get out on the ramp you have supplied for hedgehogs. If you are more worried about your fish, there is no need to be concerned. Cats very rarely catch fish, although they are fascinated by water and will sit for hours by a pond

watching what is going on there. Cats will, however, catch frogs or newts if they are on land, but there is little you can do to prevent this and it is not a common occurrence. If you just don't like cats, you will have to try to keep them out of your garden altogether.

? **There is a scum of old fish food on the pond. How do I get the fish to eat it?**

You cannot; nor should you try. Fish food should be fresh, and you should remove any old food before it rots and pollutes the pond. Stick food is one of the best types as it floats and can easily be scooped off if it is not eaten.

Clear the scum away from the pond and try giving your fish less food. You should only give them the amount that they will eat, so experiment until you find that the food is completely eaten. It is better to underfeed rather than overfeed, and fish in a balanced pond with plenty of plants will not go hungry.

6 Seasonal Maintenance

General tasks

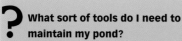

What sort of tools do I need to maintain my pond?

In reality, very few, although if you visit a water centre you are almost certain to find endless rows of gadgets that claim to make your life easy. One of the most useful items is something that you probably already have – an ordinary garden rake, which you can use for dragging weed from the pond and for removing algae. A long-handled net can be used for a number of jobs, from rescuing balls to removing leaves and old fish food. Strong waterproof gloves are also useful for getting a hold of slippery weed (*illustrated left*).

A long pole with a hook on the end (such as a boat hook, although a hoe will do instead) can be useful if you need to remove aquatic baskets and plants from the pond. If you have to go into the pond and it is deeper than your wellingtons, a pair of waders will be useful, although many intrepid gardeners are quite happy to wade in in their bare feet. You will also need a bucket for collecting weed, and it will be useful if it has got some holes in the bottom, so that water pours out and stops the bucket from getting too heavy as you fill it with weed or excess plants. It also allows you to keep the water where it is needed, in the pond.

The usual gardening tools, such as secateurs, a hand fork and a trowel, are likely to be needed at some stage, but you will already have these for other parts of the garden.

What are the basic maintenance routines?

A pond is surprisingly simple to maintain. Your main concern, especially in summer, is to make sure that the water level does not drop too much. There will be some natural variation over a period of time, especially during hot weather or if there are strong, drying winds. If you have a pond top-up system that is connected to the rainwater outflow from the gutters there should be less fluctuation in the pond level, but in dry weather the level can still drop appreciably and you should top it

up with a garden hose. Another important maintenance routine is to remove any rubbish – leaves or dead vegetation (*illustrated above*), for example – that starts to collect in the pond.

All water plants need care, but no more than those in the rest of the garden, and in fact they often require less attention. Divide them from time to time to prevent the baskets becoming choked, and remove any plants that are becoming rampant.

Some seasonal tasks are described on the following pages, but you are unlikely to have to do all of these every year.

? What happens to the pond when I go away on holiday?

Your pond will be perfectly all right for a couple of weeks while you are away. Top up the water level before you go away to make sure it does not get too low, and tidy up any plants that are beginning to go over.

If you regularly feed the fish in your pond, ask a neighbour to feed them for you but on alternate days – every day isn't really necessary. It is almost inevitable that they will be more generous than you.

Spring

? When is the best time to replant water plants?

The best time for both planting and replanting water plants is in late spring or early summer. This is when the water is beginning to warm up and the plants are just coming into growth. Any plants dealt with at this time will immediately start to grow away. If you do it in autumn the divided plant sits in water and has no chance to establish itself and may easily rot.

? Do I need to clean out the pond every year?

No; ponds rarely need cleaning out more often than once every five years (and sometimes not even that often), and a large, well-balanced pool may not need to be cleaned for ten years or more. Frequent cleaning upsets the natural balance that has been achieved. If you are careful about removing leaves and other detritus from the bottom of the pond, which you can do without emptying it, your pond will function perfectly well for many years. Do take care that you do not accidentally puncture the liner when you are removing debris.

Tasks for spring

- Clean out the pond if necessary
- If you did not do so last autumn, check that the pump, light and filtration systems that you removed for winter storage are in good condition
- Lift and divide overcrowded plants and remove all dead foliage
- Carry out any replanting
- Introduce new plants
- Be ready to protect vulnerable new growth from late frosts
- Remove any dead vegetation that was not removed in autumn
- Add barley straw to prevent algae
- Check rampant plants by removing excess growth
- Make sure there is a plant such as *Lemna* (duckweed) to cover the water's surface before the waterlily leaves have developed
- Check that no damage occurred during the winter and make any repairs that are necessary
- Feed the fish as they become active

? How do I empty my pond?

The most likely reason for you to empty a pond is so that you can repair it, and it is probable that it will be partly empty already. Reduce the water level a bit by siphoning or pumping the water out. It is possible to attach a garden hose to some models of fountain pump, but it is just as easy to siphon off water if the pond is higher than the surrounding garden.

Take out the fish (*see below*) and continue to empty the pond. If you are using a pump be careful that it does not clog up with the silt during the final stages. Put the plants in buckets or trays of water in the shade. Use a bucket or bowl to scoop up the last of the water. Work quickly: your aim should be to keep the pond empty for as short a time as possible so that you can get the fish back into their natural environment.

Use a spade (never a fork) to remove the mud and debris from the bottom of the pond, and place this on a large groundsheet or sheet of polythene near the pond. Check it before it has a chance to dry out in case there are any fish in it. The detritus can later be added to your compost heap.

the fish as you can before you take out any more water and before the mud gets stirred up. Begin to pump out or siphon off the water and transfer some of the oxygenating or floating plants to the temporary pool to provide cover for the fish. As the water level drops you should be able to net the remaining fish. If the fish in the temporary pool look as if they are in distress – gulping for air, for example (*illustrated above*), or turning on their sides – introduce an oxygenating air block of the kind used for aquaria or run a small fountain to aerate the water.

? What happens to the fish when I clean the pond?

The welfare of your fish will be your first priority if you need to empty or clean the pond, and because this is usually done in spring or early summer you must take special precautions if it is a warm, sunny day. Have a temporary pool ready for them – a child's paddling pool will do or use several clean, plastic washing-up bowls or buckets – and make sure it is in a shaded position. Siphon off or pump out some of the water from the pool and put it into the temporary pool to minimize the shock to the fish. Net as many of

? How do I clean the liner?

Once the pond is empty, remove all leaves and rotting vegetation as gently and carefully as you can with a hand trowel or small plastic scoop. Save some of this debris to return to the clean pond to help the fish become reacclimatized. Brush the surface of the liner to remove the dirt and algae that have adhered to the sides and bottom of the pond, and wash this away with clean water from your garden hose. Siphon this water away and inspect the surface of the liner in case it has been damaged (see pages 132–3). Then refill the pond.

Summer

 How do I know what are weeds and what are good water plants?

Most of the plants you buy from reputable aquatic centres and garden centres should be proper water plants, although some of these might be rampant growers, which are not ideal for a small pond (see pages 82–3 and 84–5).

If you have moved into a new house with a pond in the garden and are uncertain what to keep and what to get rid of, collect a few samples and compare them with the plants offered for sale in your nearest aquatic centre. You could always ask for advice at the same time. Just because a plant has taken over the whole pond doesn't mean it is a bad plant. (In many ways, it could be considered a good plant as it has found its right niche and is doing well.) It may simply not have been cut back for many years and can be controlled with a little care.

On the other hand, there are some plants – *Typha latifolia* (bulrush, *illustrated above*) is one of them – that are best removed from ornamental ponds, and you will have to be ruthless about removing them so that other, more desirable plants have space to grow.

Can I top up my pond with tapwater?

Yes; tapwater can be used, although the best source of water for a pond is rainwater. If possible, connect all gutters from the house and other buildings, such as sheds and garages, to the pond so that this regularly tops up the level.

It is not always possible to do this, of course, either because of the difficulties of getting the water to the pond or because there has been no recent rain. In these circumstances there is no reason not to use water from the mains.

Tapwater often contains quite high concentrations of minerals, which means that if you top up the pond regularly these will promote the growth of algae, and it is also often colder than the water in the pond. So that you do not disturb the fish, trickle the tapwater in slowly and gently, adding it every evening if necessary – little and often is better than large quantities once a week.

How can I control pests and diseases that affect the plants in and around the pond?

All plants are subject to pests and diseases at some time, and aquatic plants are no exception, although most of the common problems make the plants look unsightly rather than actually killing them.

Using chemicals to control the pests and diseases is difficult if there are fish in the pool, and you should use biological controls whenever possible. Many pesticides are harmful to fish and even if you are treating plants around the edges of the pond, some of the residue may leach into the water.

The fish themselves can be included among your control methods because they will eat insects that are washed from the plants' leaves by a jet of water from a hose.

Tasks for summer

- In early summer put out tender or marginally tender plants that have been overwintered under cover
- Top up water levels in periods of drought
- If necessary, use an algaecide to control algae and remove filamentous algae by hand
- Pull out any excessive growth of submerged or floating plants
- Remove any overgrown marginal plants
- Dead-head plants regularly to stop self-sown seeds colonizing the pond
- Weed the bog garden
- Feed the fish regularly
- Keep an eye out for pests and diseases

You can, but it is best not to, because the effect may be devastating on fish and other wildlife. As with pesticides, even a small amount of a weedkiller added to the water could be fatal. Wherever possible, weed by hand. It is never a good thing to use weedkillers among established plants because no matter how careful you are, there is always the chance that a small amount of spray will drift, and this can weaken if not kill nearby plants.

If you don't mind using chemicals in your garden, try to restrict the use of weedkillers to when you are clearing ground for the first time. If you do this properly and then keep up a good maintenance routine, you need never do it again. If it is really necessary to use a chemical herbicide, check with your local garden centre to find out what is the safest formulation to use.

No; there should be no need to renew the water each year. Indeed, it is best if you leave the water as it is, topping it up if necessary. Even if the water is cloudy and filled with algae, draining and refilling the pond with fresh water is unlikely to cure the problem (see pages 126–7). The only time that you may need to change the water is if you pollute the water – if the lawn mower falls into the pond and fills it with oil and petrol, for example.

The simplest and most effective way is to make sure that there is a good selection of submerged, oxygenating plants in the pond (see pages 80–81). Even if your pond is usually well supplied with oxygen for fish, in hot,

thundery weather the warm water sometimes absorbs oxygen less efficiently, and you may see the fish gulping for air. This can be more of a problem in a small pool than a larger one, which will have a greater surface area from which oxygen can be absorbed and zones of cooler, deeper water. Spray the water with a garden hose (*illustrated above*) or turn on the fountain if you have one. Alternatively install a small air block, available from aquatic centres, to pump bubbling air into the water.

? How can I cut the grass up to the edge of the pond?

If the problem is that the grassed area slopes towards the pond, making it difficult to control the lawn mower, you should consider levelling the surface of the lawn near the pond and supporting it so that it does not slump. This involves building a more solid bank, usually out of bricks, stone or concrete blocks (*illustrated right*), and you may have to

dismantle part of the pond to achieve this. Another problem is that grass clippings often fall into the water and are difficult to clean out properly. Unless you are keen on having grass right up the very edge of the pond, have a mowing edge of one or two rows of paving slabs between the pond and the grass.

Edging for a formal pond

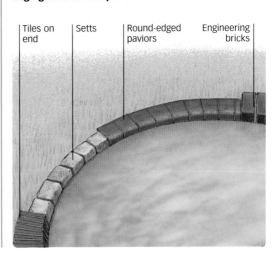

| Tiles on end | Setts | Round-edged paviors | Engineering bricks |

Autumn

? What should I do about the leaves of deciduous trees and shrubs that fall into the pond?

It is important to do all you can to keep fallen leaves out of the pond because they will decompose, making the water fetid, and eventually make the pond silt up. There are two basic ways of preventing leaves entering the pond. You can cover the whole pond with light netting for the period of leaf-fall. The net can simply be draped over the pond, although it is better to support it with a few poles placed across the pond or even on a specially made framework.

The alternative method is not so effective but it does not prevent access to the water. Here you place the netting around the pond (not over it) by creating a low fence. Use chicken wire supported on bamboo canes or sturdy posts. The leaves blowing across the garden will be trapped against the wire, and you can collect them up to make leaf mould. This method is no use if the leaves are falling from nearby trees with branches that are immediately above your pond: this is why it is best to site your pond away from trees in the first place.

If you cannot manage either of the above, you will have to clear the pond of leaves at least once a day using either a rake or net.

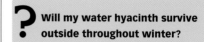

? Will my water hyacinth survive outside throughout winter?

Eichhornia crassipes (water hyacinth) is unlikely to survive in an outdoor pond, but you can overwinter it if you have a greenhouse or conservatory where the temperature does not fall below about 15°C (59°F). Take some mud from the bottom of the pool and put it in a shallow tray; you could also use soil-less compost. Take the opportunity to divide the plant and choose some healthy-looking offsets. Set these in the compost, which must be kept wet. The plants will survive over winter and can be returned to the pond when the water begins to warm up again in spring.

? What happens to the waterlilies in autumn?

Unless you have planted some tender waterlilies (see pages 90–91), you should allow your waterlilies (and any other deep-water aquatic plants in your pond) to die back naturally in autumn. You will notice that as the foliage decomposes it leaves a rather oily-looking film on the surface of the water. Removing the leaves by hand as soon as they begin to go yellow is the best solution, but you can get rid of the oily film by laying sheets of newspaper on the surface of the water. The paper absorbs the oil, together with any other debris, such as dust and pollen, which is too light to sink to the bottom of the pond.

Tasks for autumn

- Remove tender plants for overwintering under cover
- Take cuttings of marginally tender plants as an insurance against winter loss
- Cut back and remove dying stems, foliage and flowers
- Keep falling leaves out of the water
- Cut back any plants that are damaged by early frosts
- Give the fish a pre-winter boost with a high-protein feed before you begin to reduce the amount of feed you give
- If the pump will not be used in winter, take it out and clean it
- If you live in an area with mild winters, leave the biological filter in place because algae can continue to grow in winter

Winter

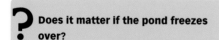
Does it matter if the pond freezes over?

If there are no fish in your pond, it does not really matter if the pond freezes, but you should take steps to stop it freezing solid. If you have fish and other wildlife in the pond, you should try to stop the entire surface being covered with a layer of ice, which can lead to a build-up of noxious gases in the water beneath the ice. Ice can also damage the liner and possibly even crack a rigid preformed liner or a concrete pond as it expands.

If you want to keep your pond free of ice you can cover it with a sheet of plastic bubble-wrap but make sure that there is some ventilation under it, perhaps by removing it briefly if the temperature rises in the middle of the day.

A more reliable method is to install a permanent pool heater, which floats in the water. It is run by electricity and will keep a small area of the water free of ice. If a layer of ice does form, melt it by holding a pan of hot water on the surface of the ice until it has melted. Never, ever try to break the ice with a hammer: the shock will kill the fish.

If you have a concrete pond or one made with a rigid preformed liner protect it by placing a few blocks of polystyrene or large, air-filled balls in the water. These will compress and take up the expansion as the water freezes, relieving the pressure on the sides of the pond.

Ice can also ruin pumps and fountains if they are near the surface. These should be drained down and stored if necessary.

? When my pond freezes in winter, how do I know when it is safe to walk on?

Never walk on your pond when it is frozen. Even if the water is relatively shallow you could still hurt yourself if the ice gave way. Apart from any injury that you might inflict on yourself, the extra pressure on the ice could well damage the pond liner and lead to leaks.

? Does ice harm fish?

In temperate climates the temperature rarely falls so low that a pond is frozen solid: there is usually at least some water at the bottom. The ice itself will not harm the fish, but the cover of ice over the surface of the water prevents harmful gases from escaping and the water can become poisonous. Try to keep at least a small area of water ice free so that the noxious gases can escape (*see opposite*).

? My pond lies at the bottom of the garden, which is in a frost hollow, and the water always freezes in winter. Is there anything I can do?

You can take the steps outlined opposite to alleviate the problems of ice once it has formed, but it might also be possible to raise the temperature in the entire area so that the water is less likely to freeze. The problem is usually that cold air rolls down the garden and collects against a fence or hedge at the bottom. If the ground continues to slope away after it leaves your garden, thinning the hedge or making some gaps in the fence will allow the cold air to continue its way down the hill, leaving slightly warmer air, enough, perhaps, to prevent the pond freezing quite so regularly.

? Can I use my fountain in the winter?

If you live in an area where the temperature remains below freezing for long periods it is sensible not only to turn off the fountain but also to drain and store the pump. However, if you experience freezing weather only very occasionally each winter the fountain can be used, but do remember to turn it off if very cold weather is forecast.

The other problem in winter is wind, and if you turn on the fountain when the wind is gusting very strongly, the water may be blown out of the collecting pool. If you run a submersible pump when it is not covered in water it will be badly damaged.

Tasks for winter

- Remove tender and pygmy waterlilies undercover
- Drain pumps and fountains that may freeze
- Leave the fish undisturbed on the bottom of the pool
- Raise the level of the pump (if it is left in the pond) so that it recirculates only the colder surface water and not the warmer water in which the fish are overwintering
- Check the surface of the pond for ice in cold weather and stop an unbroken layer of ice forming over the entire area
- Install an electric pond heater if you live in a very cold area
- Feed the birds

General problems

? How can I fill in my pond?

If you want to get rid of the pond for good the best thing is to remove the liner completely, otherwise it may become a nuisance in the future. If you want to leave the liner *in situ* but to use the area for planting, you will have to puncture the liner so that water can drain away, or it will gradually fill up with water when it rains and become unpleasant and smelly. Puncture the liner all over the base – if it is a rigid, preformed liner this can be difficult, but a garden fork will go through a butyl liner – add a layer of drainage material and top it with good quality loam. Alternatively, make a bog garden (see pages 28–9).

? Oil from my son's bicycle got into the pond. How do I get rid of it?

This is a difficult problem and is surprisingly common, although the traces of oil are often the result of accidents with the lawn mower. Even a single drop will spread across a large area of water, and the problem will appear worse than it is. Placing a few sheets of newspaper across the surface will take up most of the oil, and if it is just a trace, it will eventually disappear on its own, without causing too much damage.

If the oil produces a thick layer – if, for example, you have accidentally dropped a can of car oil in the water – it is a different matter. Your first priority should be to rescue your fish, and in these circumstances putting them in a clean container with tapwater may be the lesser of two evils. Stand the container in the shade and make sure that you aerate the water (see pages 118–19). It may be possible to skim the oil off the surface by slowly drawing a length of wood across the pond. As a last resort you will have to empty the pond, thoroughly wash down the liner and all the plants and then refill it with fresh water (see pages 114–15).

If there is a lot of water involved and you have to empty the pond, you should get advice from the local authority about the safest way to dispose of the polluted water, because you cannot simply empty it straight into the main drainage system.

? Can I build an island in my pond?

Although it will involve quite a lot of work, building an island in an existing pond is not difficult, provided you are certain that the base of the pond is safe and will not give way under any additional weight. You must also make certain that the island is well cushioned with geotextile underlay so that nothing in its construction pierces the bottom liner. Ponds made with a rigid preformed liner will rarely be large enough for an island to be incorporated, but here, too, the base must be protected with some underlay.

You will need to drain the pond to undertake the construction work. The simplest way is to build a solid surround, of brick or stone, which will have to be constructed on a foundation of concrete. The concrete should be laid as a raft over the complete area of the proposed island if it is small enough or as wide footings if the

Floating islands

An easier alternative in an existing pond is to create a floating island. This can be as large or as small as you want, but is basically a wooden raft that is anchored to the bottom of the pond.

island is to be large. A cheaper and quicker alternative is to build up the banks of an island with sandbags, arranged in overlapping courses as if they were bricks. This may not look very elegant where it breaks the surface of the water but it could be faced with logs or even planks of timber to make it look more attractive where it is visible.

If constructing a clay or natural pond from scratch it is comparatively easy to create an island as you simply leave a raised area in the middle when you are digging and then puddle the clay or lay bentonite geotextile over the area in the same way as you do to make the sides of the pond. If the banks of the island are likely to be eroded, face them with timber or stones. Plants will also help prevent erosion.

7   Troubleshooting

Discoloured water

? I have some green slime in my pond. What is it?

Of all the problems that arise in a pond, algae is the worst. It is not all bad news, because algae produce oxygen, they provide food for a number of fish and other creatures, and they use up a lot of the nutrients that come in with tapwater. Problems arise, however, when the algae get out of control and take over the whole pond (*illustrated below*). There are numerous sorts of algae, usually green but also red and blue, but the two main kinds found in garden ponds are the free-floating algae, which make the water look like green soup, and the filamentous kinds, which form mats and are commonly known as blanketweed.

A well-balanced pond is less likely to be troubled with algae, so try to achieve a balance of plants and animals, avoiding an over-preponderance of one or other elements, especially fish. An over-supply of nutrients in the water is one of the main causes of too much algae, and using rainwater rather than tapwater for filling and topping up the pond will help to reduce the level of nutrients. Try to prevent too much decaying material getting into the pond by preventing leaves from trees and leaves and flowers of marginal plants falling into the water and being left to rot. Make sure that there are submerged plants in the pond; these take up nutrients, depriving the algae of their food. Algae also depend on sunlight, so plants such as waterlilies, which cover part of the surface of the water, will reduce the amount of sun entering the water.

It is also often suggested that barley straw in the water helps to control algae. One conventional small bale to about 25,000 litres (6,600 gallons) of water should be sunk in the pond in spring. Cover it with a piece of hessian or netting to stop bits of straw floating to the surface. Smaller pads of barley straw are available for smaller ponds. No other type of straw appears to be effective.

Some of the non-strand algae can be removed by adding a filtration system to your pond. These systems either have mechanical filters where the water passes through sand or some other medium, or employ ultraviolet light, which will kill off the algae (see also pages 60–61).

? My pond is full of blanketweed. How can I get rid of it?

Once a large amount of filamentous algae has built up in the water it is more difficult to control. One of the best ways to remove it is to lift it out with a spring-tined rake; take great care that you do not damage the liner. Some people prefer to twist the algae

will clear. If the water is disturbed in any way the clay may return and make it cloudy again. Movement of water is the most likely cause of this. This may be due to a waterfall or stream or it may be caused by fish or birds searching for food on the bottom of the pond.

? The water in my pond looks milky. What has gone wrong?

Milky water is caused by the decomposition of organic matter, and the culprit is likely to be a high proportion of rotting leaves and stems on the bottom of the pond. If you have a small pond or even a pond created in a half-barrel there may be something unpleasant, like a dead frog or toad, in the pond. If you can, completely clear out the pond (see pages 114–15); otherwise, change about a quarter of the volume of water several times.

? Why is the water in my pond brown?

The most likely reason is that the mud at the bottom of the pond is being stirred up by fish. If you have a small pond with a preformed or flexible liner, this is unlikely to be a problem unless a layer of mud has been allowed to build up over the years and you have introduced fish, such as koi, that enjoy exploring the sediment. The discoloration is not harmful, and in a wildlife pond it will provide a more congenial environment for pond visitors and inhabitants than crystal clear water.

The brown colour is caused by the suspension in the water of minute inorganic particles. If you want to clear the water, you can add chemicals, known as flocculating agents, which will cause the particles to sink to the bottom of the pond. The problem will recur, however, unless you do something to stop the mud in the bottom being disturbed.

round a long forked stick, but this is slow and you will never get it all out this way. Algicides are available; these must be used with great care and only as a last resort. You will have to work out the volume of water in your pond, and you must follow the manufacturer's instructions to the letter or you will kill everything else in the pond.

Finer algae can be removed by a filter (see pages 60–61). Whatever else you do, do not drain the pond and start again. Not only will bits of algae be left on the sides of the pond and on the plants, which will soon recolonize the fresh water, but if you fill the pond with tapwater you will be providing a pond full of the nutrients on which algae thrive. Once you have removed as much algae as possible by hand, try to develop a balanced pond by following the measures outlined above.

? I have just filled my clay pond and the water is cloudy. Will it clear?

Clay ponds often remain cloudy for some time after they have been constructed, with fine particles of clay held in suspension. These will eventually sink to the bottom and the water

Overgrown plants

? **I have just moved house and the old garden pond is completely full of plants. What should I do?**

If you can identify the plants as weeds or rampant water plants, the best plan is to remove everything and start again. If you think that some of the plants are desirable and will be worth saving, remove them from the pond and divide and replant them. Check each plant carefully to make sure that it is not harbouring any weeds or you will start the process off again. The best way to do this is to wash off all the soil around every plant and to use fresh aquatic compost for every single plant.

You will probably be able to see which are the most rampant plants, and it may be a good idea not to reuse these, even though, because they have done so well in taking over the pond, these are the very plants that will thrive in the type of pond you are trying to clear out.

Whether you keep them all or not, when you are planning the replanting make sure that you have a balance of plants and that you include some submerged, oxygenating plants as well as marginal and deep-water plants.

? **My pond has become overcrowded. How do I reduce the number of plants?**

Begin by reducing the number of thuggish and rampant plants in the pond. Remove these altogether if you can and restrict yourself to plants that take up less room.

Even these better behaved plants may grow too big occasionally and need to be thinned out, but this is a necessary part of all gardening.

? **My pond is covered with duckweed. How can I get rid of it?**

This is a problem that confronts many pond owners, and it is particularly frustrating because *Lemna* (duckweed, *illustrated above right*) comes and goes: some years it will be no problem at all, then other years you will find that your pond looks as if someone has spread a bright green carpet over it.

Duckweed is difficult to eradicate completely because the plants are so small, and no matter how carefully you try to remove it, some bits always stick to other plants and will start the cycle off again.

Skim the duckweed off the surface of the pond with a garden rake. It will be easier if you choose to do it on a day when there is a

stiff breeze, which will blow most of it into a corner of the pond from where you can scoop it up much more easily.

Another way is to drag a board slowly across the pond, so that you pull all the weed into one place. With care it can also be hosed into a corner, from which it can be more easily removed.

Although duckweed should be introduced with caution, in a small pond, from which it can be netted off, it can be useful early in the year when it provides cover before waterlily leaves have developed.

By limiting the amount of sunlight that can penetrate into the water it helps to prevent algal growth. Duckweed is also a useful green food for fish and provides cover for them while they are spawning.

> **?** Self-sown bulrushes have appeared in my pond and established a colony, which is expanding steadily. Should I remove it all or just cut it back?

Typha latifolia (bulrush) and *T. angustifolia* (lesser bulrush) are far too large for most garden ponds, and you should get rid of them altogether.

Not only do the plants spread indefinitely once they are established, but the rhizomatous root system can penetrate flexible liners, leading to leaks which will be very difficult to fix.

If you have a large, natural pond you might be prepared to put up with the vigorous growth, because they are certainly attractive plants and provide valuable cover for visiting wildlife. You will have to be prepared to reduce the number of stems and underwater shoots each spring by wading into the pond and pulling them out.

This will restrict their advance into new territory and keep the plants limited to a smallish area. Be warned, however: if you forget to do it one year the pond may be filled with them by the next.

Unsuitable plants for flexible liners

In addition to the large species of *Typha* (bulrush), a small garden pond with a flexible liner is not a suitable home for *Sparganium erectum* (syn. *S. ramosum*; burr reed), which grows to 1.5m (5ft) tall, or for *Phragmites australis* (syn. *P. communis*; common reed), which grows to 3m (10ft) tall. Not only will both plants spread indefinitely, but they have strong, questing roots, that can damage flexible liners.

Neglected ponds

? **There is an old pond in the garden that is full of rubbish. Can it be restored?**

There is no reason why a neglected pond should not be restored, especially if it appears to be holding water, but the one problem with a pond that has been unattended for any length of time is that if the water level has been allowed to drop the liner may have been weakened by exposure to sunlight. This is particularly true of some of the older types of flexible liner, which were widely used before butyl became popular.

It will generally be easiest to empty the pond completely before you set about any restoration work. This will give you the chance to see what the problems are, as well as making it easier for you to work. Be careful not to damage the liner, especially if you have to walk on it. Remove all the rubbish from the pond, along with any plants that are still in their planting baskets. Drain the water; if the pond is higher than the rest of the garden, siphon it off, but if it is on the same level and you do not have a pump you will have to do this the hard way. Clear out all the other plants and scrape out all the silt and mud that has accumulated in the bottom (put this on your compost heap). Wash down the pond thoroughly, using a brush to clear away the grime and algae and using a garden hose to wash down the sides. Clear out the dirty water. You may have to repeat this process several times.

Inspect the liner for signs of tears or cracks; see pages 132–3.

If you want a pond with a layer of soil across the bottom, then get hold of some fresh loam. Do not use any of the material you have cleared from the pond and do not use ordinary garden soil, which may be filled with weeds. Refill the pond when you have finished.

? **My waterlily always produces a lot of leaves, some sticking out of the water, but it doesn't flower. Should I get rid of it?**

When waterlily leaves begin to thrust themselves out of the water it is a sure sign that the plant is in need of division and repotting. A failure to flower (or the fact that the flowers are smaller or paler than they used to be) is another sign that your waterlily needs attention.

All waterlilies, both tender and hardy, will benefit if you remove the old, inefficient roots and plant up young growth into fresh aquatic compost from time to time. Lift the waterlily from the pond in late spring or early summer and wash off the old compost from the roots. Use a sharp knife to cut off the outer, fresh branches of the rootstock and plant them up in the new compost. Discard the old, central part of the rootstock.

? **A shrub has grown so that it is overhanging my pond, which means I can't see the other plants. Should I take it out?**

This will depend on the type of shrub. Some, such as forms of *Salix* (willow), can be pollarded to the ground. They will soon put on new growth, although it may be several years before they get too large again, when you can simply repeat the process. Many other shrubs can be cut back, although not quite as severely as willow, but if it is a shrub that cannot be cut back without either killing it altogether or permanently spoiling its shape, consider taking it out and replacing it with a bush or shrub that can be pruned. Some evergreen shrubs – *Kalmia*, for example (*illustrated left*) – take many years to recover from hard pruning, but some of the forms of *Cornus alba* (red dogwood) are grown for their colourful winter stems, which are best cut back hard every year.

Pondside shrubs and trees

The following shrubs and small trees are particularly appropriate for growing near a pond in a small garden. Remember, if you are planting a new tree or shrub near a pond, to position it so that it does not cast permanent shade across the water; in the northern hemisphere this means planting it on the northern side of the pond. The dimensions below are given in the form height × spread.

- *Alnus incana* 'Pendula' (grey alder): 10 × 6m (30 × 20ft)
- *Betula nigra* (black birch, river birch): 18 × 12m (60 × 40ft)
- *Cephalanthus occidentalis* (button bush, button willow): 2 × 2.5m (6 × 8ft)
- *Cornus alba* (red dogwood): 3 × 3m (10 × 10ft)
- *Cornus stolonifera* (red-osier dogwood): 2 × 4m (6 × 12ft)
- *Kalmia latifolia* (calico bush, mountain laurel): 3 × 3m (10 × 10ft) (illustrated below right)
- *Populus* × *candicans* 'Aurora' (grey poplar): 15 × 6m (50 × 20ft)
- *Salix caprea* 'Kilmarnock': 2 × 2m (6 × 6ft) (illustrated above right)
- *Sorbus vilmorinii*: 5 × 5m (15 × 15ft)
- *Staphylea holocarpa* (bladder nut): 3 × 6m (10 × 20ft)

Leaking ponds

? **I have a pond with a flexible liner, and it seems to be leaking. How do I repair it?**

If the liner is of butyl it is well worth making the effort to repair it, and this can be fairly easily done with a patch. Other types of flexible liner are less easy to repair. PVC, for example, becomes very brittle with age and exposure to light, and there is little point in trying to repair a PVC liner that is more than about ten years old.

Whatever the type of liner, you will have to empty the pond to below the level of the damage. Clean the area around the tear with water and a scrubbing brush and allow it to dry. Apply some alcohol (such as liquid lighter fuel) to a soft cloth and wipe the area. Rubber repair kits, not dissimilar to bicycle repair kits, are available, and adhesive patches of double-sided tape can be used for small holes. If you have some offcuts of the original liner left, you can use a special adhesive to patch the damaged area. A larger tear may require the use of a heat gun to weld on the patch, and welding is often the most satisfactory way to effect a repair, although it is not necessarily

the easiest or quickest. Consult your water centre to find out what is the recommended method for your particular liner. Leave the pool overnight before refilling it.

? **My rigid fibreglass pool is leaking. Can I repair it?**

It is possible to repair a fibreglass liner, but the damage is likely to have been caused because a section of the liner was not properly supported in a bed of sand or sifted soil – the sand might have been washed away in heavy rain, for example – or because it was not perfectly level in the first place and the tension on the liner from the weight of water caused it to shift slightly and crack. Unless you can remedy the underlying cause and make sure that the unit is firmly supported and perfectly level, it will hardly be worth repairing.

As with all repairs the key is to prepare the surface. Scrub it with a brush and water, and then wipe it with a solvent, such as liquid lighter fuel, on a piece of soft, dry cloth. Abrade or score the surface around the hole to roughen the surface. Mix a two-part resin compound and apply it to the repair. If it is only a small hole this may be enough, but it is better to apply a piece of glass fibre matting that covers the hole. Both

Reparing a butyl rubber liner

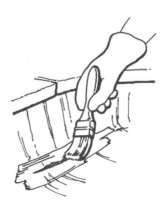

1 Thoroughly clean the damaged area. Make sure it is free from all dirt, otherwise the patch will not stick properly

2 Sand the area around the puncture to roughen the surface and, using a paintbrush, spread adhesive on and around the puncture

3 Spread one side of the patch with glue. Once both the surfaces are tachy, place the patch over the puncture and press it down

the resins and matting are readily available as
car repair kits. Fibreglass can be very sharp, so
take care. Leave the pond for about 24 hours
before refilling it.

**? Can I do something to stop my clay
pond from leaking?**

It is usually much more difficult to detect
leaks and holes in clay ponds than in ponds
lined with other materials. The leak may be
caused by roots passing through the clay or
by a piece of wood – even a stick – that has
become embedded in the clay. If you can
locate the fault the repair itself is not usually
difficult: press some soft, wet clay over the
affected area and ram it down firmly.

Cracks can also occur, but these are only
likely if you allow the pond to dry out, so the
first rule of maintaining a clay pond is never to
let the water level drop, or the banks will
develop cracks that may be difficult to seal.

**? There is a crack in one wall of my
concrete pool. How do I repair it?**

A well-laid and properly waterproofed
concrete pool should be the most permanent
type of water feature, but badly constructed

pools or ones in gardens where there is a lot
of land movement or subsidence may crack.
If the cause is ongoing – subsidence, for
example – no amount of repairs will cure the
problem and cracks will keep opening as the
land continues to move.

Not all problems are this severe, however,
and many cracks can be repaired. Drain the
pool and clean the area thoroughly with a
scrubbing brush and water. Although it may
seem odd, the next step is to make the crack
bigger. Cut along it with a cold chisel to make
a V-shaped groove. Carefully brush out all
traces of debris and dust (this is very
important), then fill the groove with a mixture
of 1 part cement, 2 parts sand and 4 parts
gravel. It is also a good idea to add a
waterproofing compound and an additive that
will prevent the cement shrinking as it dries
(this is readily available from builders'
merchants). Repaint the area with whatever
sealant was originally used on the surface of
the pond.

If you think that the pond has so many
cracks that it is beyond repair, consider lining
it with geotextile underlay and a butyl liner.
You will have to hide the top of the liner,
either by removing paving slabs and placing
the liner under this or by removing the top
30cm (1ft) of the concrete. Lay the underlay
and liner and then rebuild the top of the pond
with bricks or blocks so that the liner is
hidden behind it. If the cracks are not in the
base, make a hole through the concrete
before applying the liner so that water does
not become trapped between the liner and
the original concrete pool.

Problems with pumps and moving water

? The water from my new bubble fountain is only a dribble. What is wrong?

When you install the pump in the bottom of the reservoir you have an opportunity to adjust the flow to make sure that it reaches the top of the cobbles or millstone, and you can still adjust the flow if you dismantle it. However, the feature is probably operating just as it is meant to. The whole idea of a bubble fountain is that the water emerges, usually from a rock or stone, and just trickles over the surface of the stone or surrounding pebbles, with just enough water to moisten the stones and make them glisten and reflect the light. Some models have a small jet that rises a few centimetres, but often the water simply emerges from a hole in the centre of the rock.

? I have a single spray fountain, which is efficient but dull. Is there anything more interesting?

There is now an incredibly wide range of different spray patterns, varying from single jets to perfect sheets of water that look like glass domes. The sprays can be single- or multiple-tiered, and a visit to a good aquatic centre will give you a wealth of ideas. There should be sufficient variations to suit most tastes, but there is no reason why you should not experiment with your own designs.

? My fountain is just a trickle. What's gone wrong?

There are several possible reasons, but the most likely is that the intake to the pump has become clogged with mud or leaves. Switch off the power, remove the pump and clean it. When you replace it, make sure that you stand it on bricks so that it is raised above the bottom of the pond. Another possibility is that the filter has become blocked. Sometimes fine

material gets through and blocks the spray holes. If the water is from the mains and you live in an area of hard water, the spray nozzle may be clogged with calcium. This can be removed by a cleaner designed for shower heads or kettles. Alternatively, simply prick out the holes with a pin, taking care not to enlarge any of the holes. Finally, the problem could be a fault with the pump or its motor, in which case get professional help to sort it out. It might be cheaper to get a new pump than pay to have the old one repaired.

> **?** **The water splashes out of the pool below my waterfall, constantly depleting the reservoir. How can I prevent this?**

This could be a difficult problem to resolve, because it is probably caused by a fault in the design of the waterfall and the pool beneath it. However, before you start dismantling and rebuilding the feature, check the wind. If the waterfall is sited in a windy place a certain amount of water will miss the pool, especially if the fall is a tall one.

To correct this, try to divert or filter the wind – for example, you could plant a small shrub or two in an appropriate place to block it completely.

Although the overall arrangement may look attractive if there are rocks or stones in the pool on to which the water falls, this could well be the cause of your problem. Try moving the rocks around in the water to create a different splash pattern or, if you have to, remove them completely if water still splashes over the edge.

It is also possible that the pool is too small for the waterfall, although changing it will involve a fair amount of rebuilding. Increasing the width of the pool will increase the catchment area; increasing its depth will reduce the amount of splashing.

Adapting an existing feature

? Can I extend the pond with some flexible liner?

If the pond was originally made with flexible liner, you could add an additional section to increase the size of the pond, but you would have to be certain that the join of the two liners is completely watertight. One of the main difficulties of joining two large pieces of liner is to make sure that the two surfaces that will be in contact are perfectly clean, and this is not easy when one of them has already been underwater and covered with mud. Your local water aquatic centre will advise you on the best adhesive to use for a large joint.

? My rigid preformed pool looks too small in relation to my other garden features. Can I make the pond larger?

Some preformed pools are made in modular sections, and you may be able to find a compatible section that can be inserted next to your existing pool. This will involve some major construction work, and you must make sure that you do not disturb the existing pool.

If the existing pool is not modular it will be difficult to join another one to it. In theory you should be able to cut part or a whole side away and carefully do the same with another rigid liner and then fasten the two together with resin and fibreglass, but unless there are overwhelming reasons, it would be far easier to start again with a larger liner. If you simply want to have more water, rather than a single, large pond, you could make one or even two new pools close to the existing one and create a series of waterfalls from the upper one to the other two (*illustrated above*).

Extending the pond

A simple way of extending a pond with a flexible liner would be to create a second pool just below the first so that water cascaded over the rim of the first in the form of a waterfall into the second. You would then need to install a pump to take the water back up to the first pond.

? How can I convert my pond into a wildlife one?

Wildlife ponds are ordinary ponds that have been adapted primarily for the use of wildlife rather than for their aesthetic appearance, although, of course, by their very nature most wildlife ponds are very attractive.

The first change is to use plants that animals and birds will find attractive. Some suggestions are listed on pages 26–7, and you could also look at natural ponds in the countryside and see what plants are present and in what quantities. Most of these are available from specialist wildflower nurseries, either as seed or plants.

If possible, choose plants that are native to your area, because these will be the ones with which the local fauna will be most familiar, and you will attract more insects and other wildlife with them.

? **I built an informal pool but would like to change the style of my garden to a more formal layout. Can I convert my pond without having to rebuild it?**

If the shape is regular – perhaps a figure-of-eight or an oval or square – then it will be relatively simple to make the transformation. Even if the planting is informal, then it is a simple process of removing most or all of the plants so that the shape can be incorporated into the new design.

An irregularly shaped pond will be more difficult to accommodate into a formal scheme, however. If it is a large pond, you might be able to place geotextile underlay in the base of the pond and build a wall of bricks, stone or blocks within the existing walls, reflecting the shape you want.

You could then fill the space between the two sets of walls with soil and then cap with paving, gravel, formal borders or the surrounding of your choice.

There is no need to reline the smaller pond, because the existing liner is still place. If the formal pond is to be bigger than the existing pond, then it will be difficult to adapt the informal pond, and you will find it easier to replace it entirely.

? **Is it easy to extend an artificial stream?**

Streams are relatively easy to extend because they are linear, and all you have to do is add another section to one end (*illustrated below*). The new stretch can be lined with a butyl liner, welded to the previous section. Other materials can be joined with special adhesive. Leave a generous overlap between the two sections and lay the end of the lower section under the end of the upper section.

Many streams are now built of rigid sections of glass reinforced plastic (GRP). All you have to do to extend an existing stream is to buy one or two new sections from the same manufacturer and joint them together.

Whatever the material of the stream, you will also have to extend the run of pipe between the pump and the header pool at the top of the stream.

Children and safety

? I have young children. What water features are safe?

Children (and adults) can drown in very shallow water, and if you have young children safety will be a priority. Open expanses of water are obviously dangerous, and you may want to put off having a water feature at all until your children are older. You could construct a sandpit, which could be sited in a sunny position on or close to your patio, in full view of the kitchen or sitting room window: just the kind of position that you might choose for a small pond later on.

In some water features the water itself is hidden from view. Pebble and millstone fountains, for example, offer the attractions of water – the sound, sight and moist atmosphere – with the least possible opportunity for drowning. The body of water is contained in a reservoir, which is safely concealed beneath the feature, while a pump forces a trickle of water upwards so that it can fall over the pebbles or millstone before disappearing back into the reservoir, from where it is recirculated by a small submersible pump. These features do not have accessible pools of water, and although children can still get wet or slip on the pebbles, they should be safe from drowning.

? We have young children and have just moved into a house with a pond. Is it best to fill it in while they are young so that we can reuse it later?

It is possible to fill in a pond completely and use it as a flowerbed, but the main problem with this is that it will still retain water and flood the plants whenever it rains. If you decide to do this, you will have to make

several holes in the liner which will then need repairing once you reuse it as a pond. This should not be difficult, and it will be much cheaper than building a new pond. The other possibility is to convert the pond into a sandpit (*illustrated below*) in which the children can play. Again, you will need to puncture the liner or it will rapidly become a pond again. When the children grow up you can convert it back into a pond.

? There is a family of young children next door and I worry that they might come into my garden and fall into the pond. Is there anything I can do?

The most obvious solution is to make certain that the children have no access to the pond at all. This means that all access paths must

have gates on them and these should be locked or have childproof catches on them. The area around the pond can be a turned into a self-contained area of the garden, with its own lockable entrance, and in fact this is quite a nice design feature in its own right.

It is a pity that our lives should be ruled by the risks of accidents, but the consequences of ignoring such possibilities are awful.

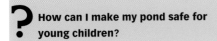

? How can I make my pond safe for young children?

There is no real way of making a pond absolutely safe except by filling it in. Children have a knack of breaking though all defences you can put up. You can put a fence round it while the children are very young to seal it off. The fence could go right round the pond or it could be used as a barrier to the section of the garden in which the pond is sited. Be sure, however, to have locks on any gates giving access to the pond.

Alternatively, you could cover the pond with a strong, rigid metal mesh held in a frame. Rather than using utilitarian chicken wire, you could make a decorative feature of the grid (*illustrated above*). If the pond has ledges around the sides, the frame can rest just below the water's surface. Alternatively, it can rest on the ground over the pond.

If you have a pond in the garden you should never leave young children alone in it. Keep a constant eye on them. Do not even pop indoors for a few minutes to answer the phone: that is when accidents invariably happen. If you must have a water feature in a garden with young children, choose one that has no open water, such as a bubble fountain or Japanese deer scarer.

INDEX

Page numbers in *italic* refer to the illustrations

A

acidity, pH levels 85
Acorus calamus 21, 96
  A. gramineus 'Pusillus' 18
Alchemilla mollis 92, 93
algae 13, 77, 126, *126*
  causes 93
  filters 61, 126
  tapwater and 117
  ultraviolet clarifiers 61, 126
  water plants and 80, 84
algicides 127
Alisma plantago-aquatica 96
alkalinity, pH levels 85
Alnus incana 'Pendula' 131
amphibians 106–7
Anubias afzelii 90
aphids, waterlily 99, *99*
Aponogeton distachyos 85, *85*, 96
Aruncus dioicus 92
Astilbe 54
  A. × *arendsii* 69, 77
autumn maintenance 120–1
Azolla filiculoides 79, 82, 83, 90, *90*

B

balconies, water features 59
Baldellia ranunculoides 96
bamboo deer scarers 58–9
barrels, half-barrels 18, 56, 81
baskets, planting 84, 89, 94–5, *95*
beaches 54–5, *55*
bentonite 35, 46, 47
Betula nigra 131
biological filters 61
biological pest controls 117
birds 26, 27, 67, 108–11
blanketweed 126–7
Blechnum spicant 93
bog gardens 28–9, *28*, 76
  construction 44–5, *44*
  liners 44
  plants 29, 88
  and ponds 29, 44–5
  shapes 28
  soil 44, 45
  stepping stones 72–3
borders: edging ponds 54, 55
  growing water plants in 76–7
brick edgings 52, *53*
bridges 72, *72–3*, 75
brimming urns 62–3, *63*
bubble fountains 134
buds, turions 97
building ponds 30–57
bulrushes *see Typha*
Butomus umbellatus 21, 97
butyl rubber liners 38, 39
  filling ponds 43
  formal ponds 20
  repairing 132, *132*
  streams 68
buying plants 77

C

cables, electricity 10–11, *10*, 60, 75
Cabomba caroliniana 90
Calla palustris 25, 96, 97
Callitriche 81
  C. hermaphroditica 97
Caltha 77
  C. palustris 23, 29, 89, *89*, 96, *96*
Cardamine pratensis 29, 93
Carex 25
  C. pendula 27
carpets, as underlay 41
cascades 14, 69
cats 111
Cephalanthus occidentalis 131
Ceratophyllum demersum 81, *81*
chalky soil 45, 46
children, safety 62, 138–9
chlorine, in tapwater 100
circular ponds, marking out 33
clay ponds 9, 35, 46–7, *46–7*, 125, 127, 133
cleaning ponds 114
cobble beaches 54–5, *55*
Colocasia esculenta 90
colour, waterside plants 93
composts 94, 95, 96
concrete ponds 48–9, *48*
  cracks 133
  formal ponds 20
  ice damage 122
  size of hole 35
containers 56–7, 87
Cornus alba 93, *93*, 131
  C. stolonifera 93, 131
costs 9
Cotula coronopifolia 89, 96
courtyard gardens 18–19, 64–5
cracks 133
cuttings 90, 97
Cyperus haspan 90
  C. longus 96

D

Damasonium alisma 18
damselflies 104
datum pegs 34
decking 70–1, *70–1*
deep-water plants 78, 84–7
deer scarers 58–9
depth of water 21, 22, 25
dew ponds 46, *47*
digging ponds 9, 30, 34–5
diseases 98–9, 117
division 87, 96, 97
dragonflies 26, 101, 104, *105*
Dryopteris erythrosora 69
  D. filix-mas 77
ducks 108–9
duckweed 77, 82–3, 128–9, *129*
dustbin lids 9, 56, 108

E

edging ponds *119*
  borders 54, *55*
  bricks 52, *53*
  grass edges 54, 119
  paving stones 43, 52–3, *52*, 119
Egeria densa 90
Eichhornia crassipes 83, *83*, 90, 120–1
electricity 10–11, *10*
  fountains 66, 67
  lighting 74–5, *74–5*
  pumps 60
  safety 11
  water features 59
Eleocharis acicularis 18, 21, 81
Elodea canadensis 79, *79*, 80, *80*, 81, 97
emptying ponds 115, 130
Eriophorum angustifolium 96
excavating holes 34–5, *34*, 46
extending ponds 136–7
'eyes', waterlilies 87

F

feeding fish 103, 111, 113
ferns 21, 69, 76
fertilizers 93
fibreglass liners 36, 132–3
Filipendula ulmaria 29, *29*
filling in ponds 124
filters 61, 102, 126

ACKNOWLEDGEMENTS

Executive Editor: **Emily Van Eesteren**
Editors: **Sarah Ford and Lydia Darbyshire**
Executive Art Editor: **Peter Burt**
Designer: **Stephen Carey**
Production Controller: **Ian Paton**
Picture Research: **Christine Junemann**

Photography in Source Order
Frank Lane Picture Agency/Terry Andrewartha
   81 left
   /W Broadhurst 118
   /Foto Natura Stock 103, 106
   /Michael Rose 115
   /Christine Sohns 88 bottom right
   /Jurgen & Christopher Sohns 127
Garden Picture Library/Eric Crichton 14 top, 61,
   128
   /Claire Davies 17 bottom
   /Des; Julian Dowle & David Steven
      Metamorphosis Garden for Citroen UK Ltd,
      RHS Hampton Court 1997 79 top
   /Ron Evans 76
   /John Glover 57 top
   /Sunniva Harte 19, 30, 33, 38, 41, 43
   /Michael Howes 51
   /Jane Legate 80 left
   /Michael Paul 48
   /Howard Rice 56, 83 top, 131 centre
   /Gary Rogers 22
   /Alec Scaresbrook 6
   /JS Sira 54
   /Ron Sutherland 58, 62
   /Juliette Wade 23 bottom, 72, 73 botttom, 129,
      134
   /Steve Wooster, Harpers & Queen, RHS
      Chelsea 1994 13
Garden & Wildlife Matters 46, 131 bottom
John Glover 29
   /Fairfield 108
Jerry Harpur 78, 121 top
   /Des; Michael Bolston, Wiltshire 138
   /Chanticleer PA, USA 16
   /Des; Topher Delaney, San Francisco CA 59
   /Des; Melanie Edge, London 2
   /Des; Penelope Hobhouse 52
   /Des; Tim Newbury, Cramphorsn, RHS Chelsea
      1990 92
   /Des; Mirabel Osler, Shrophire 77
   /Des; Chris Rosmini, USA 15
   /Des; Judith Sharpe, London 65
   /Wyken Hall, Suffolk 67

Marcus Harpur/Des; Christopher Bradley-Hole,
   RHS Chelsea 2000 70
Holt Studios International/Nigel Cattlin 23 top
   80 right, 93 bottom, 105 top
   /Bob Gibbon 81 right, 90 bottom
   /Primrose Peacock 63
   /Rosie Mayer 119
   /Peter Wilson 47
Andrew Lawson 17 top, 21, 85 top, 86 bottom,
   93 top, 135
   /Arrow Cottage, Hereford 66
   /House of Pitmuies, Tayside 24
   /Des; Wendy Lauderdale 25
S & O Mathews 4-5, 7 top, 7 bottom, 28, 68, 84
   left, 85 bottom, 86 top, 89 bottom, 94, 96 top,
      96 bottom, 97, 136, 137
   /Morton Manor 125
N.H.P.A./G I Bernard 101
   /Stephen Dalton 105 bottom
   /Nigel J Dennis 110
   /Martin Garwood 100
   /Hellio & Van Ingen 107
Clive Nichols 102
   /Des; Richard Coward 117
   /Des; Natural & Oriental Water
      Gardens/Garden & Security Lighting 74, 75
   /Vale End, Surrey 53
Photos Horticultural 91 Top, 91 Bottom, 99, 104,
   116
   /RHS Chelsea 1991 9
Derek St Romaine 3, 8, 12, 34, 69, 111, 112, 113,
   114, 121 bottom
   /Des; Nigel Boardman & Steve Gelly, Garden
      Circles, RHS Hampton Court 2000 87
   /Des; Paul Butler & John Roberts, RHS Tatton
      Park 1999 18
   /Des; Garden Gang and David Brun, RHS
      Hampton Court 2000 20
   /Des; Rachel Hardwick, RHS Hampton Court
      1998 71
   /Des; Mr & Mrs Hickman, Little Lodge 82
   /Des; Robin Templar-Williams, Help the Aged,
      RHS Chelsea 2000 139
Harry Smith Collection 14 bottom, 31, 36, 37,
   40, 44, 57 bottom, 73 top, 79 bottom, 83
      bottom, 84 right, 88 top left, 89 top, 90 top,
      98, 120, 122, 126, 130, 131 top
   /RHS Garden, Rosemoor, Devon 64